Personal Learning Aid for

The Art of Writing Clearly

Personal Learning Aid for

The Art of Writing Clearly

W. G. Ryckman

Coordinating Editor
Roger H. Hermanson
Georgia State University

DOW JONES-IRWIN
Homewood, Illinois   60430

ISBN 0-87094-388-X

Printed in the United States of America

1 2 3 4 5 6 7 8 9 0 K 0 9 8 7 6 5 4 3

PREFACE

Julius Caesar called one of the tribes he conquered barbarians because they had no money to use as a medium of exchange, constructed no permanent buildings, and had no system of writing. Our culture is much different: money turns the wheels of commerce; brick, concrete, and glass are transformed into imposing structures; and writing covers millions of acres of paper. Desks are inundated with it, hundreds of thousands of file cabinets bulge at the seams, men and women spend lifetimes wading through tons of letters, reports, and memos.

The vast majority of this paper is produced by business—public, private, and institutional—and the pity of it is that for the most part the words inscribed on it have been difficult to write and are even more difficult to read with understanding. This book has been written with definite purposes in mind: to make writing a less distasteful task and to offer suggestions that will cause what is written to be more clear as well as easier for the reader to comprehend.

Worthy purposes, we will agree, but to accomplish them it is essential that my writing be clear, concise, and convincing. You will have to be the judge of my success in this respect.

So, let's get on with it.

W. G. Ryckman

TOPICAL OUTLINE
OF COURSE CONTENT

CONTENTS

THE USE AND MISUSE OF WORDS

1

The wise writer knows the meaning of the words he uses. If he is not certain he has chosen the right word, he checks it in the dictionary. Should he be unable to find it, he should realize that the word does not exist or he is not spelling it correctly. Either conclusion warrants the choice of a different word.

Mrs. Malaprop was a mistress of the art of picking the wrong word for the right occasion. She had a knack of using a word that sounded almost like the one she should have selected. For two centuries theatergoers have chuckled at "like an allegory on the banks of the Nile," but how many corporate presidents chuckle when they read the minutes of a directors' meeting and find that "the meeting was *adjoined* at four o'clock"? Have you ever seen an ad in the Help Wanted section of the newspaper that starts: "Stock Clerk—High *Renumeration*"?

Here are a few more tricky pairs of words:

Accept—Receive.	Except—Everything else but.
Adapt—Adjust to new use.	Adopt—Use, take as one's own.
Advice—Counsel.	Advise—Give advice.
Affect—Influence.	Effect—To bring to pass (verb), result (noun).
Allude—Make indirect reference to.	Elude—Avoid adroitly, escape.
Appraise—To evaluate.	Apprise—To give notice, tell.
Capital—Capital letter. Capital assets. Principal. City serving as seat of government. Part of a column. Capitalism.	Capitol—A building in which a state legislature meets or in which the U.S. Congress meets.

The House and the Senate meet in the *capitol* (that big building on the hill) at the *capital* (Washington).

Compliment—An expression of esteem, respect, a flattering remark.	Complement—To complete, make perfect.

Epithet—A short descriptive word or phrase. Richard *the Lionhearted*.

Expletive—An oath. Also *It* in, *It* is a sure thing.

Farther—Refers to distance

Further—Refers to time or quantity.

Imply—Suggest indirectly.

Infer—Draw meaning from data.

I *infer* from your *implication* that . . .

It's—Contraction of *it is*.

Its—Possessive of *it*.

It's a thrill to hear a bird sing *its* song.

Less—Refers to quantity.

Fewer—Refers to number.

Fewer people have learned to talk *less*. An unclear but fascinating concept.

May—Permission granted. You *may* take a leave. Perhaps, uncertainty. I *may* take a leave.

Can—Implies physical ability to take an action.

Perimeter—Boundary, length of a boundary.

Parameter—A word with a very specialized meaning. It is <u>not</u> a synonym of perimeter. Look it up before using.

Principle—A basic rule or truth.

Principal—Number one in rank. Capital as distinguished from spending money.

Verbal—Using words, written or spoken.

Oral—Uttered by mouth.

One hears the words *verbal agreement* used to describe two parties coming to terms without committing the deal to writing. If it had been written it would still be a *verbal agreement*, wouldn't it? So, don't say *verbal* when you mean *oral*.

ADJECTIVES

Picking the right adjective can be a problem. According to the grammarians an adjective is a word serving as a modifier of a noun to denote a special quality of the thing named, to indicate its quantity or extent, or to differentiate a thing from something else.

Examples of the three types of adjectives:

A *famous* man
A *full* cup
The *fourth* son

No problem so far, but what about choosing the proper adjective to convey the writer's precise meaning? Take the familiar word *famous*. It is a catchall with a number of more specific synonyms that can be used to capture the exact meaning in the mind of the writer. For instance:

Famous—(*a*) Widely known, (*b*) honored: an unspecific general word.

Celebrated—Implies more notice and attention, especially in print: a *celebrated* actor.

Renowned—Implies more glory and acclamation: a *renowned* author.

Noted—Suggests well-deserved public attention: a *noted* authority.

Notorious—Adds an implication of questionableness or evil: the *notorious* Jesse James.

Distinguished—Implies excellence or superiority: the *distinguished* judge.

Eminent—Greater than distinguished.

Illustrious—Implies enduring honor and glory attached to a deed or person: Thomas Lincoln's *illustrious* son.

To call Abe Lincoln *notorious* or Jesse James *illustrious* would be improper. We are told that Winston Churchill, in writing a speech, changed one adjective eleven times before he found the one that expressed his exact meaning.

Poets and writers of flowery prose use adjectives to add color and imagery to their writing. Authors of business communications should be restrained so they will not allow their rhetoric to carry them away. From our childhood days we have sung ". . . by the dawn's early light . . . ." *Early* is redundant. What other kind of light could the dawn provide?

The business writer should use as few adjectives as possible. The major trouble is that most of them are imprecise and convey no exact meaning. Take this sentence: "Pin-Up Corporation expects to earn _____ profit this year." Fill in the blank with one of the following adjectives, adding an article if necessary:

Acceptable	Low
Adequate	Nominal
Appropriate	Reasonable
Average	Slight
High	Small
Inadequate	Some
Large	Substantial
Little	Unacceptable

Each adjective may have a different shade of meaning from all the others, but the reader is forced to make the decision as to what the word means to him. No two readers can be expected to agree on the definition of what is *adequate*.

If the writer expects Pin-Up to earn $850,000, let him say so and allow the reader to decide if this amount is *adequate, substantial, reasonable,* or whatever. Of course, the writer who commits himself to a precise figure must answer to the consequences if he proves to be wrong, but he is paid to be right and should not be allowed to shirk his responsibility by using weasel words. Avoid the use of vague modifiers; always be as specific as you can.

ADVERBS

Adverbs are first cousins to adjectives—they modify verbs, and adjectives modify nouns.

The man ran *quickly.* The adverb *quickly* relates to the verb *ran.* Many adverbs end in *ly.* Some modify an adjective: She wore a *beautifully* tailored jacket.

So much for the mechanics of adverbs. The same rules apply to adjectives and adverbs alike. Be sparing of them in your writing, and when you employ one be sure it is the right one.

Now let us consider two pairs of words: *bad* and *badly, good* and *well*. For such small words they take as much abuse as any others in the English language.

Bad is an adjective; *badly* is an adverb.

He is a *bad* boy. (*Bad* relates to *boy*, a noun.)

I played *badly*. (*Badly* relates to *played*, a verb.)

You would never say, "He is a *badly* boy," but millions upon millions of people say, "I played bad." Shame on them.

Good is usually an adjective; *well*, an adverb.

He is a *good* boy. (*Good* relates to *boy*, a noun.)

I played *well*. (*Well* relates to *played*, a verb.)

Simple, isn't it, yet you never watched a weekend golf tournament on TV without hearing an announcer or a millionaire golfer state, "He hit it real good today." If, instead, he hit it *really well* would he have incurred a two-stroke penalty?

It is a strangely human quirk but many people judge their peers by how well they employ their native tongue. Careless and slovenly errors in grammar can turn off such people. Why take the chance of offending someone who may be important to you?

FOREIGN WORDS AND PHRASES

Don't spice your writing with an overabundance of foreign words or phrases. They sound ostentatious and should be used only when there is no equal substitute in standard English.

An *ad hoc* committee is one formed to perform a single specific service. The president of a company may be, *ex officio*, a member of a company committee. In other words, his membership is due to his position.

Both of these Latin phrases are acceptable as they have become familiar to most of us, and it is difficult to coin an equivalent, concise English phrase.

There is a very real distinction between Americanized foreign words and those that still maintain their foreign flavor. Only the latter group should be avoided in business writing. Examples of Americanized foreign words:

Détente

Delicatessen

Matinee

Résumé

Other words are familiar to most of us; some of them have been Americanized, but they still sound foreign. Since there are even more familiar substitutes we can use, we should choose them in preference to the foreign word. Examples:

Don't write	When you mean
Bête noir	Bugbear
Bona fide	Authentic, sincere, in good faith
Caveat emptor	Let the buyer beware
En route	On the way
Faux pas	Blunder
Gratis	Free
Naïve	Artless, credulous, natural
Nouveau riche	New rich
Parvenu	Upstart
Raison d'être	Reason for existence
Sine qua non	Essential thing

The phrase *hors d'oeuvres* is in a class of its own. It conjures up a vision of caviar, red and black, smoked salmon, artichoke hearts, anchovies coiled on melba toast, and all sorts of delicacies. *Appetizer* is a pallid substitute, but I suggest that in conversation, at least, you stay with *appetizer* until you are absolutely certain of your pronunciation of *hors d'oeuvres.*

Words flow back and forth across oceans and frontiers, and in the course of time become citizens of the countries they invade. Consider these words:

Chassis	Garage
Chauffeur	Landau
Coupe	Limousine
Detour	Tonneau

One might almost suspect the automobile had been invented in France rather than in Detroit.

A good rule to follow with regard to foreign words and phrases is to use them only if they have been Americanized or if there is no readily available substitute in American English.

A BRACE OF PERSNICKETY PAIRS

Two words often misused are *literally* and *figuratively*. The former means strictly realistic, whereas the latter refers to an imaginative, not an actual, action.

He *literally* frothed at the mouth.

The person about whom this statement was made either suffered some type of seizure or had ingested soap powder with the result that he actually did froth at the mouth.

He was so angry that, *figuratively*, he breathed fire and brimstone.

Such an act could never be called *literal* unless the individual referred to was either a dragon or one of those Indian fakirs who swallows and then exhales fire.

The other often misused pair is *among* and *between*. In their most common usages *between* denotes a relationship between two things, *among* when there are more.

He was *between* the devil and the deep blue sea.

He was *among* a host of enemies.

BUSINESSESE

Young executives attempt to impress their peers and especially their superiors by their mastery of a vocabulary composed of what, in business schools, are called *buzz words*. Many of these are excellent words when properly used, but most of them are pallid substitutes for words better suited to the purpose. A few are colorful and descriptive. For example, *bottom line*, meaning the result, is more pleasing to the ear than the *net, net* it has replaced. Yet, Thomas Jefferson did not say that the *bottom line* was "life, liberty, and the pursuit of happiness."

Implement as a verb is much overused. The dictionary does dignify its use, but when policies, programs, actions, and practices are *implemented* a half dozen times a page, the reader feels he has been bludgeoned with a blunt implement and has been exposed to the inane ramblings of an ignoramus.

So many *scenarios* are being *orchestrated* in business communications, one might feel all corporations are engaged in fitting musical accompaniments to filmed epics.

Enterprising authors are now marketing books containing lists of hundreds of jargon words with which bosses will be impressed, and aspiring executives are being told that fluency in this new language is a prerequisite for a successful career. Ridiculous.

At some point in time has been an enduring favorite of the aficionados of businessese. I presume we are to visualize time as extending from here to there, and if we make a mark with a pencil between the two limits (parameters to some misguided souls), we have established *some point in time*. Why not use *at some time* or *when*?

Impact, improperly used as a verb, is another favorite of the jargoneers. *Impact* is a good verb; it means to fix fairly, to press together, or to impinge upon. Agreed, but it is not proper to say, "Rising costs will impact profits." Rising costs will *reduce, affect,* or *lower* profits; they will never *impact* them.

Here is a short list of businessese words. More are being coined daily, and you should feel free to make continuing additions. An occasional use of some of them is not a heinous crime, but overuse is to be avoided.

Bottom line	Input	Rewarding
Challenging	Interface	Scenario
Dialogue	Linkage	Synergy
Dichotomy	Meaningful	Throughput
Feedback	Orchestrate	Thrust
Frame of reference	Output	Track record
Hopefully	Parameter	Value judgment
Implement (v.)	Relevant	Viable

GOBBLEDYGOOK

When convoluted syntax and tortuous sentence structure are super-imposed on a plethora of businessese jargon, the result is *gobbledygook.*

This word is found in dictionaries and can be defined as "wordy and generally unintelligible jargon." Its spawning ground is the swampy wastes of barren bureaucratic cranial vacuums. (Not bad as an example of amateur gobbledygook.) As far back as World War II a blackout order was phrased this way: "Obscure fenestration with opaque coverings or terminate the illumination." It would never do to have said: "Pull down the shades or turn out the lights." In a simpler vein, when an aspirant threw his hat into the presidential ring, a commentator referred to the act as a "meaningful threshold for a viable campaign."

Here is an example of gobbledygook in its most advanced and purest form. "It has been decisioned," wrote the commandant of the Marine Corps, "that some form of unit rotation may be a desirable objective. . . . Recent CMC decisions have alleviated the major inhibitors allowing a fresh approach and revaluation of alternative methods of unit replacement."

I object to: *decisioned.* What's wrong with *decided?*

I object to: *may be a desirable objective.* The CMC should be capable of deciding whether it was or wasn't desirable. CMCs, I hope, are men of action, not wafflers.

I object to: *alleviated the major inhibitors.* Why not *made it possible?*

I object to: *fresh approach and revaluation.* Redundant. Why not *review?* (One positive note: the CMC did not write reevaluation.)

What regulation would the CMC have violated had he written: "It is now possible and desirable to review various methods of unit replacement." I hope the CMC did not close his statement with a request to be *copied* with all *interreactions* to his directive.

Strive for clarity. Don't use long words when short ones will do the job better.

Don't use	When you can use
Circumvent	Avoid
Currently	Now
Defunct	Dead, out of business
Eternal vigilance	Alertness
Finalize	Finish
Forfeit	Lose
Increment	Growth, increase
Initiate	Start
Minimal	Least
Perimeter	Limit, bound
Periphery	Rim
Peruse	Look over
Preponderant	Chief
Rescind	Call off
Subsequently	Later
Unavailability	Lack of
Unequivocal	Certain
Utilization	Use

Maslow has his hierarchy of needs, and many workers extend his theory to job titles. One utility employee, a meter reader by trade, thought he should be referred to as a Utility Data Recording Technician. The title would be more impressive. For some reason his employer didn't see it his way.

USE OF LATIN ABBREVIATIONS

Suggestion: Don't use them.
Exception: When clearly superior to alternatives.
Example: Dodgers v. Giants. It is not easy to find a suitable substitute for *v.*

Don't use	When you can use
cf.	Compare
e.g.	For example
et al.	And others
etc.	And so forth
i.e.	That is
re or in re	About, concerning
viz	Namely

CLICHÉS

I have a happy recollection of Jimmy Demaret doing a TV commentary on a golf match some years ago. As I remember, he said something like this: "Jack, wielding his trusty Texas wedge, canned a snake from the froghair." Sports heroes have been known to tarnish their images when they open their mouths. Baseball players are no exception to this generalization. How often have you heard the slugging outfielder say: "He'd been tossing up junk and breaking stuff, you know, but I waited for his high hard one, and when it came, uh, I went with the pitch, got good wood on it and rode it to the opposite field seats, you know what I mean." In other words he hit it *good*.

Practicing athletes and jock broadcasters who have been boning up on Ring Lardner are not the only murderers of the King's English. Businessmen are equally bitten by the cliché bug. Instead of a stale cliché, use a fresh, direct word.

Cliché	Substitute
As a matter of fact	(Leave it out)
Despite the fact that	Although
Explore every avenue	Analyze
In accordance with	By, following
In most cases	Usually
In the last analysis	(Excise the phrase)
On the grounds that	Because
Strive with might and main	Try
The foreseeable future	The future (who can foresee the future?)
To my knowledge and belief	I know
To tell the truth	(Redundant. We assume you always tell the truth)
To the best of my ability	(Forget it. We assume everything you do is to the best of your ability)
With the result that	So that

SLANG

There is no place for slang in business writing. Prose can be dignified without being pompous or stilted. Individuals should never be referred to as *this guy* or *that fellow*. *Ain'ts* should be reserved for dialogue in short stories.

Going down the tube, meaning approaching bankruptcy, is a colorful expression but more fitted to a business school classroom than to a business communication.

Today, when we are *between a rock and a hard place*, we stoically *bite the bullet*. Reserve such histrionics for describing your emotions as you reach for your wallet after blowing a six-foot putt on the last green to lose the match.

Jokes, coarseness, and profanity should be avoided in formal writing. The person you offend may be the one individual you can't afford to upset.

Contractions should be avoided. Spell out all words fully. Never write:

Can't	I've	Isn't	We've
Don't	Shouldn't	It'll	Won't

QUIZ

Circle the appropriate word to fill the blanks.

1. Inflation will _____ corporate profits.
   affect or effect
2. He _____ the impact of inflation on profits.
   appraised or apprised
3. I cannot walk any _____ .
   further or farther
4. They shook hands to seal their _____ agreement.
   oral or verbal
5. _____ fun to see a ball team play _____ best.
   its or it's
6. Both teams played _____ .
   good or well
7. He _____ made an ass of himself.
   literally or figuratively
8. What is the preferred shorter substitute for:
   a. Forfeit   _____
   b. Currently   _____
   c. Preponderant   _____
   d. Utilization   _____
9. Replace the abbreviations with suitable words.
   a. etc.   _____
   b. i.e.   _____
   c. in re _____
   d. cf.   _____

10. What would you write to replace the following clichés?
    a. In most cases   _____
    b. On the grounds that   _____
    c. With the result that   _____
    d. To my knowledge and belief _____

ANSWERS

1. Affect.
2. Appraised.
3. Farther.
4. Oral.
5. It's, its.
6. Well.
7. Figuratively.
8. a. Lose.
    b. Now.
    c. Chief.
    d. Use.
9. a. And so forth.
    b. That is.
    c. About, concerning.
    d. Compare.
10. a. Usually.
    b. Because
    c. So that.
    d. I know, I believe.

THE UBIQUITOUS "I"

I find I lose my patience when I read too many *I*'s, *my*'s, and *we*'s. A few are all right, but there is no excuse for half a dozen a page. Overuse of the vertical pronoun is a stylistic solecism only, but it should be avoided.

A problem might arise if you are directed to give your personal opinion on a subject. You might be inclined to commence in this fashion: "I recommend we buy the company. In arriving at my decision I examined costs, probable profits, and availability of capital. I did not feel it appropriate to consider legal implications as these are outside my area of control." Couldn't it be reworded as follows: "I recommend we buy the company. The decision was based on an examination of costs, probable profits, and availability of capital. Legal implications were not considered as these are outside my area of control."

Two *I*'s and a *my* have been eliminated with no weakening of the text. You will note the first *I* was not tampered with. The active *I recommend* is much stronger than the passive *It is recommended*, and the positive note struck by the *I* lets the reader know that the writer is taking full responsibility for his recommendation.

Careful editing should eliminate the personal pronoun problem.

I AND WE

An insurance company declines to issue a policy. Does the employee who relays this information to the client start his letter: "I regret I cannot . . ."? Does he write, "I regret we cannot . . ."? or does he phrase the decision this way: "We regret we cannot . . ."?

The English would call the quandary a sticky wicket and for good reason. When the writer uses two *I*'s as in the first example, he implies that he and he alone made the decision. He assumes full responsibility for the refusal. It is highly unlikely that a single individual, unless he holds a position of awesome authority, can unilaterally decide the issue on his own. He is probably guided by explicit company policy and in all likelihood has discussed the matter with a colleague or superior. Thus, to write, "I regret I cannot . . ." is neither candid nor totally accurate.

"I regret we cannot . . ." is much better. The *I* is a personal touch that might mitigate slightly the disappointment of the client on receiving the news. "We regret we cannot . . ." is colder, more impersonal.

All of us are familiar with the editorial *we*. We recall our amusement at the royal use of the pronoun by Queen Victoria when she said, "We are not amused." For those of us who are neither editorial writers nor empresses, the word *we* usually refers to the organization that pays our niggardly salaries, whereas *I* refers to personal opinion. Thus: "I am concerned with the weakness in new car sales, and at General Motors we . . ."

Do not, by the use of *I*, assume authority not fully vested in you.

Is it all right to write: "I regret we cannot issue the policy, and I suggest that you . . ."? I think so. The company has turned down the client; you personally are sorry and suggest an alternative action. I find nothing wrong in that.

Consider for a moment the use of *I* and *we* in reports. "I recommend we commence construction of the new plant immediately." It is the writer's opinion that the company should build the plant. Executives are constantly being asked their personal opinions, decisions, and conclusions. Replies should include the pronoun *I*, but when action ensues, the corporate *we* should be used.

COLLECTIVE NOUNS

A company or a corporation is an *it*, not a *they*. A baseball team, though composed of nine members if we ignore the designated hitter which we and the game should do, is still an *it*. The theory behind this, I suppose, is that a company or a team is a group and as such is singular.

Few of us would use a plural verb when referring to a group. "The company *are* going to introduce a new product" sounds offensive to the ear as well as to our grammatical sense. But a goodly portion of us frequently err when we replace *The company* with a pronoun. We write or say, "*They* are going to . . ." instead of "*It* is going to . . ."

So far, so good, but here is where the waters become muddied. "The Steeler team leads the league." But, "The Steelers lead the league."

Hardly news. In the first statement the verb is singular because the collective noun *team* is singular, and in the second the plural verb refers to the players on the team rather than to the organization itself.

In short, when the group or organization is referred to, a singular verb and pronoun should be used. When individuals that make up the group are discussed, plural forms should be used.

REDUNDANT OR UNNECESSARY WORDS

No author worth his salt can go peacefully to his heavenly reward if he has not at frequent intervals in his career delivered a number of pungent aphorisms on the subject of redundancy in writing. Basically, they all express similar sentiments; to increase the power of his work, a writer would do well to strike out every second, third, or fourth word of what he has written. Unfortunately, not one of them tells us which words should be excised, and to me, that is the secret of the tightening process.

There can be several types of redundancy. Irrelevant material is redundant; so are unnecessary words and superfluous adjectives and adverbs.

In the chapter devoted to editing, more is said on the subject, so at this point (I should have used *now* and saved two words) we will discuss two stylistic aspects of redundancy.

Never use several words when one will do the job. Why write *despite the fact that* when you can write *although*, or *in the majority of cases* when *usually* means the same thing? Tenth graders, when assigned a theme of two hundred words, use such circumlocutions to reach the desired number. Businessmen should have different objectives. Never use more words than necessary to express your thought. Examples of wordy expressions and their equivalents:

Aforesaid	(Don't use)
As to whether	Whether
At the present moment	Now
Due to	Because
For the purpose of	For
Hold a discussion	Discuss
In depth analysis	Analysis
In view of	Because or since
In view of the fact that	(Even worse)
On a formal basis	Formally
Should it transpire that	If
Take action	Act
Take notice	Notice or note
With respect to	About, concerning

Another cause of redundancy is a lack of understanding of the precise meaning of a word. Take *unique*, for example. It means single, sole, without like. How then can anything be *very unique*? *Consensus of opinion* is another clinker. *Consensus* says it all on its own as it is defined as group solidarity in sentiment and belief.

Here are more expressions of the same ilk:

Deeply profound	Occasional frequenter
End result	Successfully convinced
Exactly identical	Successful triumph
Fellow colleague	Surrounded on all sides
Fully competent	Total ban
Important essential	Unexpected surprise

TECHNICAL SUBJECTS

A geologist writing a memo to others of similar training will use a technical vocabulary fully understandable to his peers. When he addresses a reader not familiar with the terms and expressions of his field, however, he would be wise to couch his statements in words understandable to intelligent people who have no specialized training in geology.

Marketeers talk to each other using terms such as *rollout, skimming, market segmentation, pull* and *push* promotions. Such terms might mystify the parent company's treasurer who was being asked for a substantial increase in the advertising budget.

POLYSYLLABIC PROLIFERATION

The use of long, awkward, or unfamiliar words does not impress the reader with your erudition. On the contrary, he will be turned off if he feels you are deliberately trying to expose his illiteracy. Avoid verbal blockbusters. Keep it short and sweet.

Not long ago I came across a curious combination of letters in a piece of writing; "mneumatic." No such word exists, but the dictionary suggested the writer may have had one of these words in mind:

Pneumonic—Having to do with the lungs.

Pneumatic—Inner tube or buxom burlesque queen effect.

Mnemonic—Aid to memory—from Mnemosyne, Greek goddess of memory and mother, by Zeus, of the nine Muses. A fascinating character.

None of these words made much sense in the context of the writing, but during my research I happened upon the longest English word I have ever seen. It relegates antidisestablishmentarianism, a puny twenty-eight letters, to the junior varsity.

Pneu-mo-no-ul-tra-mi-cro-scop-ic-sil-i-co-vol-ca-no-co-ni-o-sis.   A lusty forty-five letters that describe a disease of the lungs caused by inhaling quartz dust. Which means more to you, the forty-five[1] letter word or the definition?

A more concise example of the wrong word in the right place is an excerpt from a recent news article describing the scene of a gang killing. "_____ was on the floor, the top of his head blown off and a cane-backed chair resting precipitously on his leg." How can an article at

---

[1] Numbers twenty-eight, forty-five, and forty-five have been spelled out as this is not a financial report containing many figures, and the numerals 28, 45, and 45 would appear to be out of place. See the following section, Numbers.

rest, in this instance a cane-backed chair, be described as *precipitous*? I wonder what the reporter was trying to say and what the rewrite man was dreaming when the story crossed his desk.

The moral to this is: Don't use a combination of letters that cannot be found in a dictionary and don't use an unintelligible blockbuster when easily understood shorter substitutes are available.

NUMBERS

Eleven million, nine hundred sixteen thousand, five hundred thirty-seven dollars, and sixteen cents. Fourteen words! Why not $11,916,537.16? Spelled out numbers take more space and are much more difficult to comprehend than numerals.

Yet, "The proposed energy program will cost approximately $142,000,000,000." The eyes are boggled as well as the mind. When I see a number like that, I start at the right and say, "Hundreds, thousands, millions, billions," as I count each set of three zeros. Isn't *$142 billion* easier to read and equally effective?

A treasurer's report to his board will employ a number of figures. He will probably use numerals solely. Another report may have only three numbers in it: 28, 45, 45. A better appearance might be achieved if the three simple figures were spelled out.

A savings bank will advertise 5½% interest on passbook accounts. To write *five and a half percent* would neither attract the eye or impress the mind. Either *10%* or *10 percent* is preferable to *double digit* in profane reference to inflation rates.

A rule of thumb followed by many newspapers is to spell out numbers through nine and use numerals from 10 up.

What have we decided about writing numbers? As I started to write this section, I thought I knew my . . . (No! Three *I*'s already and one *my*—rewrite.) I am convinced that . . . (No! Beware of phrases such as this.) Let us put it this way. There are no hard and fast rules covering writing numbers. Consider appearance and ease of comprehension, save as much space as possible, strive for clarity, and be as consistent as possible. Do not write *four* on one line and 5 on the next. Finally, whatever you do, do it for a reason—consider the alternatives first and adopt the best method of writing your numbers.

Having said there are no firm rules to cover number writing, I will now hedge. To start a sentence with numerals is definitely wrong. "1066 was the year of the Norman invasion." Either spell out *Ten sixty-six* or reword so the date appears later in the sentence. "The Norman invasion occurred in 1066."

MINOR IRRITANTS

The word *prejudice* covers acres of ground. One definition calls it a preconceived judgment or opinion not supported by facts or reason. I want to tell you about a few of mine in the next page or two. Perhaps *prejudice* is not the right word to describe my eccentricity; Idiosyncrasy comes closer. (Two very long words to describe a feisty testiness of nature.)

One of my strongest hang-ups is directed at those memo forms that thousands of businesspeople use. Across the top is the heading *From the Desk of* and below it is the printed name of the proprietor of the piece of furniture sending the message.

When I was an office denizen and received one of these missives I had a compelling urge to direct my reply to the desk. Why it should be concerned with the matter at hand was a mystery, as was how it proposed to act on my reply should there be one.

Couldn't the form be headed *Memo from . . .* ?

Another of my favorite hang-ups is directed at people who advance an argument and then say, "*As you can clearly see.*" Nobody tells me what I can clearly see. Perhaps my glasses are dirty or misplaced and I can't even see the end of my nose clearly. I may be asked to look, but I and I alone will determine what I can clearly see. Even that isn't right. It should be *see clearly,* not *clearly see.* The same goes for *it should be evident that . . .* , *I am sure you will agree that . . .* , and similar effronteries. One must be able to enjoy one's foibles. If you can't, what is the point in nurturing them?

Let us return to the *From the Desk of* form for a moment. We must accept the conclusion that this is the *personalized* era. (Dear me, I have done it myself. I have no right to tell you what you should or should not accept. The sentence must be revised. "To me, the present is characterized as the *personalized* era." That's better even if the sentence does contain two *ized* words. My apologies.) We are surrounded on all sides (another slip—eliminate *on all sides,* or change to *we are beset on all sides,* please) by *personalized* towels, sheets, stationery, luggage, cuff links, pens and pencils, shirts, ad infinitum, ad nauseam. (Use of Latin phrases not generally recommended but perhaps acceptable in this questionable attempt at whimsical humor.) *Personalized* means only that one's name or initials appear on the article. Say that, if you must, but use of the word *personalized* is not to be tolerated. (My final solecism. Passive construction is weak; active is strong. Rephrase. ". . . but avoid the use of. . . .")

To find one's writing so poor is discouraging, especially when one has the presumption to set himself up as an arbiter of writing style. This brief digression points out the insidious nature of the traps that await a writer. Maintain eternal vigilance. (Shouldn't I have said, "Be alert"? Why us three long pretentious words when two short snappy ones would do better?) Sharpened, blue, editing pencils are essential for writing vigorously, clearly, and concisely. (Note the three modifiers of *writing* and a like number for *pencils.* Use nouns and verbs—be sparing of adjectives and adverbs.)

As I write these words, my ear is tuned to the early morning radio news. Within the space of three minutes I have heard a former president, in an interview, say, ". . . to assure him *of the fact that* not only I but. . . ." I have heard an announcer declaim, in touting a product, "It is *very* unique, indeed." I have also heard a newscaster discussing the *scenario* of an unsuccessful space shot. He considered the incident " . . from the *people hazard* standpoint."

One is inclined to say, "Its spinach and to hell with it! If you can't beat em, join em." (Come, come, my friend. The contraction of *it is* is *it's. Them,* when contracted, becomes *'em.* Amen.)

MORE MINOR IRRITANTS

Irregardless.   Never use. The word does appear in the dictionary but with the note, "nonstandard." Write *regardless* and save two letters.

Fact.   "The Declaration of Independence was signed July 4, 1776." This is a fact. "Jimmy Carter was a great president." Political implications aside, the statement is not a fact because it relies on a personal valuation. This alone removes it from the *fact* category. There is a real distinction between facts and assumptions or conclusions. Don't mistake one for the other, and make your differentiation clear.

Different than.   No. *Different from.*

Myriad.   From the Greek, meaning: (1) Ten thousand and (2) an immense number. The second definition is the more widely used. "Myriad grains of sand on the beach." Never use a *myriad of* anymore than you would refer to a *countless of* stars in the heavens.

Integrity of singular and plural.   British writers perpetrate verbal rape on our language by switching from singular nouns to plural pronouns. Horrible. The practice has osmosed across the Atlantic. Eradicate it.

"*Every man* should watch *their* step." *His.*

The orchestra saved *their* best efforts for *their* final selection." *Its* twice.

A singular antecedent requires a singular pronoun.

Very.   Use sparingly. A weak word; a useless adjective.

All right.   There is no such word as *alright.*

Anybody.   Usually one word. When written *any body,* it refers to one of several cadavers littering the premises.

Regionalisms.   The subject embraces a number of heinous sins. I refer to this type of speech or writing as *hound dog.* Individuals on whom this opprobrious epithet is hung respond with rancor. Forget them!

"Where is your car *at*?" Why not, "Where have you parked your car?" or even more simply, "Where is your car?"

"I have no doubt *but that. . . .*" Say or write, "I have no doubt that . . ." or better yet, "I am sure that. . . ."

"I *can't hardly* tell the difference." An unwitting double negative.

One regionalism is unavoidable. The English language has hundreds of thousands of words; I don't know how many. Yet, there is no way to describe the most common cause of a car coming to a stop on the highway. One person says, "I ran out of gas." Another laughs at this quaint expression and offers as replacement, "I *gave* out of gas." What can one say?

It is a strange language that we write and speak. "I woke up when the alarm clock went *off.*" In this sentence *off* means on.

I have been getting further and further away from regionalisms. You should do likewise.

Vague references and words.   A writer rambles on for a page or two and then commences a new paragraph with: "This means that . . ." Quite properly the reader asks to what does *this* refer? *It* and *this* generally require an antecedent, something that clearly identifies what the *this* or *it* relates to.

Posture. Another in-word. We must adopt a posture for everything. Military *posture*, economic *posture*, foreign relations *posture*. As a callow youth I was constantly exhorted to improve my *posture*. My mother meant stand up straight, you round-shouldered, spaghetti-backed urchin. *Posture* does have another definition; frame of mind, attitude. Granted, but be sparing of use in this context.

Vehicle. The *h* is silent, the accent is on the *v*. A yokel pronounces it *ve-hick-le*.

QUIZ

Indicate whether the following statements are true or false.

1. Contractions may be used in formal writing. _____
2. The personal pronoun *I* should never be used in business correspondence. _____
3. An organization should be referred to as an *it*, not a *they*. _____
4. A technician should use his specialized vocabulary when writing a report. _____
5. Use of very long words will impress a reader favorably. _____

Correct the following sentences.

6. There were six oranges and 12 pears in the basket.
7. 1914 saw the outbreak of the First World War.
8. Irregardless of what you say, I believe you are wrong.
9. Every person should live their own life.
10. Writing is entirely different than speaking.

ANSWERS

1. F
2. F   But be sparing in its use.
3. T
4. T and F   True if the readers are equal experts in the field; false if they are unacquainted with the jargon.
5. F
6. Either six oranges and twelve pears or 6 oranges and 12 pears. I prefer the former, but the main point is to be consistent.
7. Nineteen fourteen or rephrase the sentence to read; World War I broke out in 1914.
8. Regardless
9. His
10. From

WRITING STYLE
AND FORM

2

We have spent considerable time on the subject of words and it is now time to concern ourselves how to employ them to the greatest advantage. In doing so we will explore age-old fallacies relating to split infinitives and prepositions and touch on several types of what I call organizational punctuation: parentheses, brackets, slashes, and footnotes.

Finally we will get down to what this chapter is all about: writing style. Words are the tools of the writer's trade. The ones he picks and how he strings them together in sentences and paragraphs determines the quality of his style. There are as many different styles as there are writers and just as there are good writers and bad writers so are there good styles and bad styles. Remember your high school experiences with Addison and Steele, with Hazlitt and Lamb. I don't suppose any of us will attain the rare excellence in style reached by those essayists but at least we can be aware of some of the principles of good writing exemplified in their work.

SPLIT INFINITIVES

To knowingly or unknowingly split an infinitive is not considered good grammatical form. Many people have no idea what an infinitive is and wouldn't know how to go about splitting one. Did you spot the glaring split in the first sentence?

Just what is a split infinitive? I have researched the question thoroughly and am more confused than enlightened by my study. The dictionary is a waffler spouting bureaucratese, and even W. H. Fowler, in his monumental work, *Fowler's Modern English Usage*, spends two and a half pages attempting to explain the inexplicable. So please accept my suggestion as to a working definition of the term.

For our purpose an infinitive is a verb preceded by the word *to*. Thus: "To curse fluently is an art." *To curse* is our infinitive, and to split it, all we have to do is move *fluently* between the two parts of the infinitive. "To fluently curse is an art" contains our split infinitive.

What law have we broken and why is it such a dastardly crime? I haven't the foggiest except Miss Weller, in the sixth grade, told me I must never, never, split an infinitive. I haven't done it since.

Indeed, "To curse fluently" sounds better than "To fluently curse." The ear should be the final arbiter. "I can't force myself to actually root for the Yankees." That sounds normal; my ear is not offended, although denizens of the Bronx may not agree with my sentiments. To say, "I can't force myself actually to root for the Yankees," sounds awkward, stilted.

When you split an infinitive, be aware of what you are doing. Split it only if your ear tells you that you should. Would a complete change of sentence structure suit your purpose even better? Be your own judge, but what you do, do deliberately.

ENDING A SENTENCE WITH A PREPOSITION

A preposition is the part of speech used to relate a noun to another word in a sentence.

"He knocked on the door." *On* is the preposition that relates *door*, a noun, with the verb *knocked*.

Among the most common prepositions are:

At	Of
Before	Off
By	On
For	To
From	Up
In	With

One of the first rules of grammar I learned was that a preposition should never be used to end a sentence. Why not? No one ever told me because I suspect there is no valid reason not to. (Not bad.) There is, I agree, something unattractive about a well-rounded sentence ending abruptly with an *of*, a *to*, a *for*, or a *with*. Yet change in construction may result in even more undesirable results.

"What are we waiting for?" Would you prefer, "For what are we waiting?" I wouldn't.

But, "There are the feathers you should stuff the pillow with." No. "Stuff the pillow with those feathers." Preferable, provided one is not allergic to feathers.

"What were you thinking of?" sounds better than "Of what were you thinking?" Doesn't it?

It all depends on the ear. (Come now, what does the *it* refer to? Shouldn't I have written, "To what does *it* refer?" No way.)

Confused? Don't be. Know what you are doing, but let your judgment and your ear control what you do.

ACTIVE AND PASSIVE VOICES

Whenever possible, avoid the passive voice; it is weak, stilted, and usually leaves questions in the mind of the reader.

"It is expected that mortgage rates will continue to rise over the next quarter."

Who expects rates to rise? Why should the reader believe such a statement? "I expect mortgage rates to rise over the next quarter because. . . ." Now the reader has information on which to base his acceptance or rejection of the statement. Perhaps the writer of the first sentence was trying to avoid the use of the personal pronoun. Good for him, but in this instance the weakness of the statement is more unacceptable than the use of *I*.

Unfortunately, use of the impersonal passive has long been popular with many bureaucrats and businesspeople.

It is widely believed that. . . .
It has come to the attention of management that. . . .
It is suggested that. . . .

Users of the passive voice in phrases such as those listed above have been called pusillanimous shirkers from responsibility. Let no one hang such an epithet on you. If you believe something, don't be afraid to admit it; if you favor a certain course of action, recommend it and don't pussyfoot around.

The active voice is strong—use it. The passive voice is weak—eschew it.

SUFFIXES -IZE, -WISE, -SHIP

"We must prioritize our inputs economywise." The writer possibly means we should establish an order of importance in considering steps to effect savings. At least he did not tell us that *prioritization* is essential.

To many misguided people, adding *-ize* or *-wise* to a word sounds highly professional. We *finalize, maximize, strategize.* One of the first women ordained by the Episcopal Church said: "I will not let the church inferiorize me again." Bully for her. She certainly achieved self-actualization personality wise.

In 1940 German Panzers swept through France and the Lowlands. Today a correspondent might report: "Situation wise, inputs from France indicate maximized nonsuccess battlewise." Churchill said: "The news from France is bad."

Ize and *wise* don't add. They detract from clear forceful writing. Avoid them.

Ship is another overused and misused suffix. This morning I actually heard a radio announcer say: "Amelioration of the gas shortage has impacted in a negative manner on Metro ridership." She used the word *ridership* twice more in the next twenty seconds. (No, I am not unaware of the misuse of *impacted.*)

Each usage bothered me because the word sounded contrived, artificial. I felt very virtuous until I suddenly recalled Miss Weller, who, more than half a century ago, strove valiantly but unsuccessfully to teach me *penmanship*. A horrible word but how about *penwomanship*?

FOOTNOTES

In general, business memos and reports are not similar to academic or scientific papers in which every statement must be supported by a specific reference to its direct source. Footnotes are distracting to a businessman. They disturb the flow of his reading, especially if they are accumulated at the end of the report and he is forced to go back and forth to refer to them. Avoid them whenever possible.

Some highly technical reports will require footnotes, and they should appear at the bottom of the page below a line that clearly indicates they are not part of the text.[1]

PARENTHESES AND BRACKETS

In nearly every situation commas can be used in place of parentheses. Stay with the familiar and avoid the unfamiliar punctuation symbols. "The increase of Accounts Receivable (if it continues at the present rate) will have a serious . . ." Here commas are preferable to parentheses.

Parentheses may be used when referring to exhibits. "Costs are estimated at $450,000. (See Exhibit III.)"

Normally it is not necessary to include numerals in parentheses to emphasize a written number. "There are now fifty (50) stars in our flag." Flush the (50).

Brackets are used to enclose extraneous matter in a quotation. "*Almayer's Folly* [Conrad's first novel] was published in 1895." They are also used to enclose the Latin word *sic* when you wish to draw attention to an error in a quotation. "The dog was chasing it's [sic] tail." Whenever I am confronted by this usage of brackets, I get the impression the writer arrogantly assumes I am too ignorant to spot the mistake. A murrain on him.

EQUAL RIGHTS IN GENDER, LEADING TO A DISCUSSION OF THE SLASH

Chairman, Chairwoman, Chairperson
Mrs., Miss, Ms.
A person is entitled to his/her opinion.
Who in his/her right mind voluntarily chooses a perch between Ossa and Pelion? What man/woman steers his/her craft deliberately between Scylla and Charybdis?

Make up your own mind and do whatever you please, but include me out of the battle.

Another digression rears its ugly head. You will note the use of the slash (/) in preceding paragraphs. There, the punctuation mark was used to indicate an option. It is also employed to indicate the end of a line of poetry incorporated in the text. "The first version of Blake's 'The

Hold For
W. Blakele
5-26-87

---
[1] If you must have footnotes, use this form.

Tyger' commences, 'Tyger, tyger, burning bright/ In the forests of the night.'"

The most common use of the slash is in *and/or*. This is pure legalese. Don't use it. "Production and/or marketing are (is?) involved in the problem." The writer means that the problem involves either production or marketing or perhaps both divisions. Let him say so.

The slash is acceptable when used to designate a unit composed of several separate entities. For instance: "Sales can be expanded in Parkersburg, Wheeling or in Morgantown/Fairmont/Clarksburg." The first two cities named are separate territories. The combined area around the last three cities named would be considered as a single territory. In this example, use of the slash saves space and is readily understandable.

OVERKILL IN WRITING

In a written business communication reiteration is redundancy. Write it once, write it clearly, and then go on to the next point. Don't repeat yourself. There is a hoary old saw (mind how you spell hoary) to the effect that when making a speech, one tells the audience what one is going to say, then says it, and concludes by telling the audience what it has been told. This is fine for some speeches but unacceptable in a relatively short written report.

The written word endures forever. Once a statement is made, it need never be repeated. There is no place in a report for such phrases as "to recapitulate what I have previously stated" or "as I mentioned earlier." Say it once, say it firmly, concisely, and clearly.

To add a touch of inconsistency, in a lengthy report some concession to this precept may be necessary, but needless repetition should be avoided.

The observant reader of this section will discover that I have made a simple statement: *don't repeat yourself,* and then said the same thing in slightly different words at least six more times. How's that for consistency?

RHETORICAL QUESTIONS

Don't ask a question unless you are prepared to handle the response. I once was a member of an organization of friendly souls who/that[2] held an annual banquet at which the new slate of officers was installed. Before and during dinner spirits ran high. When the retiring president rose to introduce his successor, he planned to offer a glowing tribute to the new leader. He started with a rhetorical question? "Who is Mere-

---

[2] *Who* if referring to souls, *that* if referring to organization. Unclear. Rewrite.

dith and what has he done for us?"[3] That was as far as he got. There was a wild uproar in the audience. Shouts of "Who the hell cares," "Not a damn thing," could be heard.

The sterling character and outstanding achievements of our new president remained a deep secret. A year later Meredith did not open his speech with a rhetorical question.

In writing also, rhetorical questions are to be avoided. Don't ask a question and then answer it. That approach is a time and space waster, and it irritates the reader.

"I examined the financial situation and what did I find?" Awful. Examine the situation on your own time and tell us what you found.

"What, you may ask, will be the consequences of this law?" Rubbish. "The consequences of this law will be. . . ."

DOGMATIC STATEMENTS

Beware of overuse of such phrases as:

I believe
I think
I feel
It is my opinion

Especially beware of:

I am certain
I am positive

To be avoided at all costs:

I am absolutely convinced

If such phrases are followed by one or more "becauses," the writer should say, "I conclude" rather than, "I think." A reasoned conclusion has more weight than an unsupported statement.

Never does vehemence of language make up for faulty logic. Readers are suspicious when a writer attempts to steamroller them into agreement.

Don't be dogmatic in your Olympian pronouncements:

Everyone knows . . .
There can be no argument with the conclusion that . . .
It is an accepted fact . . .
Clearly . . .

Such statements irritate a reader and give him an opportunity to display his perverse streak. What might be crystal clear to you might not be as apparent to him. Convince him with the weight of your logic and allow him to decide if the purported fact is indeed acceptable to him.

---

[3] Ben Johnson got away with it when he wrote: "Who is Sylvia? What is she?"

┌─── **QUIZ** ──┐

Indicate whether the following statements are true or false.

1. An accomplished writer never splits an infinitive.   _____
2. Neither does he end a sentence with a preposition.   _____
3. Active voice is stronger than passive.   _____
4. In general, there should be little use of footnotes in
   business writing.   _____
5. Using suffixes such as *-ize, -wise, -ship* give writing a
   professional tone.   _____
6. It is often wise to repeat or rephrase a point for emphasis.   _____
7. Rhetorical questions can cause more trouble than
   they are worth.   _____
8. Avoid statements that are excessively dogmatic.   _____
0. The slash (/) is used to indicate an option or the end
   of a line of poetry.   _____
10. In most cases parentheses may be used in place of
    commas.   _____

ANSWERS

1. F
2. F
3. T
4. T
5. F   They accomplish the opposite.
6. F   Repetition is permitted only when argument is long and
       involved.
7. T
8. T
9. T
10. F   The opposite is true.

└───┘

SENTENCE STRUCTURE

What is a sentence? (Is it alright [sic] for me to start this section with a rhetorical question or should I have begun, "A sentence is . . ."?) The dictionary has several definitions for *sentence*, and I'll attempt to distill them into a few simple words. A sentence is a grammatically and syntactically related group of words that expresses a statement, a question, a command, wish, or exclamation. Usually it begins with a capital letter and concludes with appropriate end punctuation.

That appears simple enough but we have only scratched the surface. There are simple sentences, complex sentences, compound sentences, compound-complex sentences, run-on sentences, loose sentences, balanced sentences: their name is legion.

I have no intention of making this section a treatise on grammar. I am not competent to do so and leave the field to properly trained eighth-grade English teachers who have the most difficult and frustrating job in the world.

Let us dally for a moment, however, on the subject of sentences.

"Run!" That is a sentence according to the definition. It is one word, expresses a complete thought in the form of a command, begins with a capital letter, and has appropriate end punctuation.

"The man runs." Here we have a subject and verb.

"The tall man runs slowly." Both subject and verb have a modifier. The adjective *tall* precedes the noun *man*, and the adverb *slowly* follows the verb *runs*.

"The tall young man, clad in a jogging outfit, runs slowly along the path." Somewhat more complex but perfectly clear.

"The tall young man, clad in a dirty blue jogging outfit with green stripes, runs slowly along the rutted dirt path that winds through the beeches, oaks, and aspens of Birnam Wood." That's about as much mileage as we can expect to get out of this sentence. Any more descriptive information crammed into it would result only in confusion.

How about word order? We could have said, "Slowly, the tall man runs." The emphasis is now on *slowly*. In similar fashion we could rearrange the next sentence to read: "Clad in a jogging outfit, the tall man runs along the path slowly." Emphasis again is changed, but I don't like the position of *slowly*. It is too close to *path* and too far from *runs*, the verb it modifies.

If we alter the order of the final sentence, total confusion results and meaning is obscured. All examples are *simple* sentences, containing no dependent clauses; even so the final one is complex enough for an ordinary reader.

What does all this prove? How long or how short should a sentence be? What should be the word order? A writer should strive for variety of structure, but clarity is the primary objective. Variety is necessary so the mind and eye will not be bored by the monotony of sentence after sentence of the same length and construction. Writing style and custom have changed over the years. A study disclosed that three hundred years ago written sentences averaged about sixty words; a hundred years ago the average had fallen to about thirty. Subject matter affects sentence length. An instruction manual accompanying a "Make-It-Yourself Atom Bomb Kit" that employed sixty-word sentences to explain highly technical details of construction might trigger a premature explosion.

In 1767 Laurence Sterne wrote *A Sentimental Journey*. The reverend doctor's concept of punctuation is not as modern as his approach to what we now call situational ethics; so I shall start the excerpt with the words that follow the last period that appears in the work. To set the scene: Sterne stopped at a small inn and engaged the only bedroom which, by chance, contained two beds. In the evening, a Piedmontese lady of about thirty "with a glow of health on her cheek," accompanied by a "brisk and lively" maid of twenty, also stopped at the inn. Sterne politely offered the other bed to the lady, and a formal agreement was reached regarding the decorum of the two principals during the enforced sharing of the chamber. The sleepless Sterne, in the middle of the night, broke Article 3 of the agreement by ejaculating, "Oh, my God." The lady, apparently also suffering from insomnia, immediately charged him with a treaty violation. Now—to our sentence.

Upon my word and honor, Madame, said I—stretching my arms out of bed by way of asservation—

—(I was going to have added, that I would not have trespass'd against the remotest idea of decorum for the world)—

—But the Fille de Chambre hearing there were words between us, and fearing that hostilities would ensue in course, had crept silently out of her closet, and it being totally dark, had stolen so close to our beds, that she had got herself into the narrow passage which separated them and had advanced so far up as to be in a line between her mistress and me—

So that when I stretched out my hand, I caught hold of the Fille de Chambre's—

THE END OF THE SECOND VOLUME

One is scarcely aware that the sentence does not conclude with an appropriate end punctuation.

Let us now leap ahead to 1899 when Conrad wrote *Lord Jim*. An explanation of the situation is not necessary for understanding of this excerpt from the climax of the novel.

Jim came up slowly, looked at his dead friend, lifting the sheet, then dropped it without a word. Slowly he walked back.

"He came! He came!" was running from lip to lip, making a murmur to which he moved. "He hath taken it upon his own head," a voice said aloud. He heard this and turned to the crowd. "Yes, Upon my head." A few people recoiled. Jim waited awhile before Doramin, and then said gently, "I am come in sorrow." He waited again. "I am come ready and unarmed," he repeated.

Great writing by two masters of prose—I hope you will agree—but poles apart in many ways. Each author captures the mood for which he strives; each word has a purpose; each concept is clear. Writing like this doesn't just happen; it doesn't spring fully formed from the brain of the author.

Hemingway may unconsciously have emulated Conrad; Faulkner is more akin to Sterne in structure if not imagery. What happens to sentences when one is neither a Sterne, a Conrad, a Hemingway, nor a Faulkner?

Let us start by correcting an obvious fault. "He saw a rainbow going downtown." Rewrite. "As he was going downtown, he saw a rainbow." Eliminate the dangling participle.

"Shooting par frequently is a golfer's ambition." Does *frequently* refer to *shooting par* or *ambition*? How you write it depends on what you mean. Be sure what your modifier modifies.

"The point at which you order being your order point which is a combination of your requirements during lead time plus a buffer stock which will cover us in case of any undue fluctuations in demand."

That collection of words starts with a capital letter and ends with a period, but that doesn't make it a sentence. After two or three readings one realizes what the writer is trying to say. The trouble is he started babbling and never took himself sternly in hand. What he is attempting to tell us is that stock should be reordered far enough in advance to allow for normal use during the time between the order and the expected delivery of the order. He states also that a cushion to cover unexpected high demand in the interval should be maintained. How would you express these thoughts clearly and succinctly to your purchasing department?

If you can handle that one, try this: "Further, unless petroleum prices do not become prohibitive (which is unlikely since petroleum is not a renewable resource) plastics may not continue to make significant inroads into paper products." Here our fledgling Homer had no clear concept of what he wanted to say when he picked up his pen. He started with a vague idea and plowed ahead without ever considering where his rhetoric or his syntax was taking him.

Clarify your thoughts before you start to write and hope you will never involve yourself in a quadruple negative that defies translation into understandable prose.

Here is another gem that on the surface appears fairly easy to correct.

"The fact that all the aforementioned management owns at least some stock in the company should make for their commitment to making it a success greater than otherwise."

Prolix, convoluted, ungrammatical. Will this do? "Since all management owns stock in the company, it will work harder for its success." Simpler—certainly—but still not absolutely clear. In the original, *management*, a singular noun is properly given a singular verb *owns*. Later the writer uses *their*, a plural pronoun referring to *management*. In the revision the correct *it* is used, but this *it* is confused by the *its* referring to *company*. So: "All management, owning stock in the company, will work harder for the company's success." If we feel we should emphasize the ownership factor more heavily, we might write: "Since all management owns stock in the company, each manager will work harder for the company's success." That is probably the concept the writer wanted to get across to the reader.

Is it necessary to take a microscope to every sentence we write? I should hope not, but sentences must be examined carefully if we are to be precise in our meaning, if we are to be clearly understood. A ray of hope: If you know what point you are going to make before you start a sentence, you have a better chance of expressing it clearly.

Professional status in constructing sentences that are totally unintelligible is reserved for bureaucrats who have spent years learning the art of obfuscation. What normal mortal could coin this sentence contained in a HUD report?

"Action-oriented orchestration of innovative inputs, generated by escalation of meaningful indiginous decision-making dialogue, focusing on multilinked problem complexes, can maximize the vital thrust toward a nonalienated and viable urban infrastructure." Pure genius!

Stick with nouns and verbs. Use adjectives and adverbs sparingly. Do not string nouns together in a stately array. Do not run sentences on interminably, covering a half-dozen different subjects. Use a normal, standard English vocabulary.

PARAGRAPHS

Paragraphs make a lot of sense; I'm all for them. They serve two principal purposes: to provide the reader with a short respite and to assure his brain that two or three pages of unbroken type will not have to be slogged through before he can allow his attention to relax for a moment. Both of these points are important if a writer wishes to make it as easy as possible for his reader to follow his argument.

This defense of paragraphing is very impressive, but how long should a paragraph be and what is the rationale for determining its length?

The first rule to remember is that a paragraph deals with a single point. That statement is so important that I'll repeat it. A paragraph deals with a single point. Have you got that?

It would be entirely proper to cover, in general terms, the creation of the earth in a single paragraph. It would not be proper in one paragraph to describe in detail the specific acts performed on each of the six days it took to do the job. Each day should be assigned its own paragraph.

Remember also, although excessively long paragraphs intimidate a reader, a procession of excessively short ones, each only a line or two, will irritate him.

Attempt to combine short paragraphs, break up overlong ones, but never ignore the one-point rule.

In grammar school we learned that a paragraph should have a topic sentence—one that prepares the reader for what follows. There should also be a smooth transition from one paragraph to the next so there will be a flow of language and thought from one to the other—no abrupt change in direction, no surprises.

Successful writers of business reports use headings for the various sections of their papers. These headings, like the ones we have employed throughout this book, are great word savers. They replace the topic sentence that otherwise would be necessary. The writer, having said what was required in the section on Marketing, drops down two spaces and writes:

Production

The reader knows exactly what is coming next, and the writer can plunge into what he wants to say. It is not necessary for him to state in his final sentence on marketing that, having completed his analysis of that subject, he will now direct his attention to production.

Underlined headings serve another important purpose. They make it easy for a reader to locate a section of the report he wishes to reread, which is a great help when the report is a long one.

Internal policy in some corporations does not approve indentation of the first line of a paragraph. My preference is in favor of indentation—it does break up the monotony of a page. Also, I see no reason to double-space between paragraphs as long as they are addressing the same primary subject.

When the section on Marketing is complete, however, I do suggest dropping down two lines before writing the new heading.

Headings should be underlined using a single continuous line rather than underlining one word at a time.

Energy Requirements for the Next Decade   Yes

Energy Requirements for the Next Decade   No

Broken lines make for slow reading and poor appearance.

Use upper and lower case when writing headings, reserving all capitals for emergencies:

IMMINENT BANKRUPTCY

REFERENCE BOOKS

Two books should always be within reach of a writer: a dictionary and a thesaurus.

Use the dictionary to check your spelling and the meaning of words. Use it also as a guide to pronunciation should you fear you might have to read aloud what you have written. Few people realize the wealth of miscellaneous information contained in dictionaries.

You will find rules for spelling; for forming plurals and compounds; and for punctuation, capitalization, and italicization (quite a word). You will be instructed how to address a member of the Catholic brotherhood; you will note that the ZIP code of Cedar Crest College in Allentown, Pennsylvania, is 18104; and you will learn that Godwin Austen, also called K2, is, at 28,250 feet, the second highest peak in the world. You will also be made aware that Howrah is a city on the Hooghly River opposite Calcutta and boasts a population of almost 600,000 inhabitants.

Believe it or not, dictionaries can be fun.

A thesaurus is quite another matter. Be sure your copy is printed in dictionary form. Originally, thesauri were arranged in sections, and a word with several meanings—such as *green*—would appear in a number of different categories. As a result, a voluminous index would have to be consulted before the proper section could be located. In the *Dictionary Form* the various meanings are collected in a single listing, and synonyms are shown for each meaning. Thus, we are told that the color *green* may be described as emerald, chartreuse, jade, olive, to name a few tints and shades, and that *green* also means callow, raw, inexperienced, or youthful. In the same listing we find *green* means lawn, terrace, grass. Normally, noun, adjective, verb, and adverb forms are given.

Often one needs a synonym to eliminate the necessity to repeat the same word over and over again in a written work. An *expenditure* can be an *expense,* a *disbursement,* an *outlay,* a *waste.* At times one seeks shading in a word to express precise thought. Is a *thief* an embezzler, a *safecracker*, a *bandit*, a *robber*, a *swindler*? The thesaurus will suggest the right word.

In addition, the book is essential for a rapid (speedy, expeditious, quick, fast, alacritous) solution of the Sunday *Times* double acrostic.

Misguided high school teachers of English have been known to recommend the use of a thesaurus to students so they can use sesquipedalian (a foot-and-a-half-long) words in their themes instead of better short ones. Teachers like that should be decollated instanter (beheaded at once). Use the thesaurus, but use it for the proper purpose.

A familiarity with two other books can prove equally rewarding to anyone who is really interested in acquiring the art of good writing.

The first of these is *The Elements of Style* by William Strunk, Jr., and E. B. White. A small book, shorter even than this one, it has influenced several generations of writers and has deservedly earned the status of being considered a classic on the subject.

The other, a much more ambitious work of over 700 pages, is *Fowler's Modern English Usage* by H. W. Fowler, an erudite and, in a nice way, eccentric Englishman. I and thousands of others have spent many enjoyable hours leafing through the book, and if I have a question on grammar or usage, Fowler is always there with an encyclopedic answer.

I commend both books to you without reservation.

QUIZ

Indicate whether the following statements are true or false.

1. Sentences should vary between 10 and 30 words. _____

2. A series of long paragraphs is more desirable than a succession of very short ones. _____

3. I can recognize a dangling participle when I see one. _____

4. In developing an attractive writing style, it is helpful to restrict the number of adjectives and adverbs. _____

5. No paragraph should be an entire page long. _____

Write your answers in the space provided.

6. What are the advantages of using headings in a business report?

7. What services do paragraphs perform?

8. How much information should a paragraph contain?

9. In a few lines demonstrate your understanding of and your feelings about the use of the passive voice.

10. Write a couple of sentences on split infinitives and prepositions at the end of a sentence.

ANSWERS

1. F
2. F   Both are equally undesirable.

3. If your answer is false go back and reread the section on this subject.

4. T

5. T

6.   *a.* They eliminate the necessity for transitional sentences.
     b. They apprise the reader of the next subject.
     c. They make it easy for a reader to find a section of the report.

7.   *a.* They gather all information on one point in a single entity.
     b. They provide a respite for a reader.
     c. They don't intimidate him with pages of unbroken type.

8. As much as is needed to cover a single point. If the paragraph is excessively long, it may be subdivided at appropriate points.

9. Passive construction: It is believed that . . .
Active construction: I believe that . . .
The passive voice is weak. A user of it may be accused of shirking responsibility for a statement.

10. When you place an adverb between the word *to* and a verb, you have split an infinitive. It is no sin to do so provided the construction sounds normal and does not offend the ear.
Although a sentence may end with a preposition, in many cases it will be improved by rephrasing.

EDITING

I am reluctant to discuss this subject as I fear it will prove to be a difficult assignment. Yet editing is such an integral part of writing it cannot be ignored. Few mortals can write fluent, grammatical, forceful prose off the tops of their heads. There is a room in the British Museum where manuscripts of famous authors are displayed. A page in the handwriting of Anthony Trollope, a benign and civilized Victorian novelist, indicates he was one of the lucky few. His first draft was his finished work. Trollope was unique in that he worked not like an artist but as an artisan, assigning himself regular hours at his desk and a fixed number of pages of manuscript to be produced, depending on the press of work in his regular job and whether he had to meet a publisher's deadline. On the average he assigned himself about forty pages a week. He tells us: "And as a page is an ambiguous term, my page has been made to contain 250 words; and as words, if not watched, will have a tendency to straggle, I have had every word counted as I went." Think of that; 10,000 finished words a week, and don't forget he turned out as many as 112 pages when the need arose.

Well, as far as I could tell, there were about 250 words on the page I scrutinized and not one correction or revision marred the sheet. A page of Lewis Carroll's *Alice in Wonderland* is equally uncluttered with changes. Not so with James Joyce. He crosses out, adds, revises, adds again, deletes, changes to the point that the page is indecipherable. I am not convinced the typesetter set what he was supposed to set or that Joyce knew the difference. The revision was no more intelligible to me than the original draft had been.

One can spend a fascinating hour or two in the museum observing the workings of genius. I apologize. This digression has been rather lengthy, the purpose of which is to impress on you, gentle reader, that some few crumbs of culture have dribbled onto my waistcoat. Another reason, perhaps, is that I don't quite know how to begin a section on editing.

This time the dictionary is of little assistance. It mumbles about editing the complete works of an author, editing out, or deleting, and that's about it. Mr. Webster is probably in the same boat with me. I'll have to take a chance and do it on my own. Editing, to me, consists of ensuring that:

1. Words are spelled correctly.
2. The right words are used to express precise meaning.
3. Sentences are grammatically and syntactically correct.
4. Punctuation follows accepted standards.
5. Paragraphs are of manageable length and observe the *one-point* principle.
6. The whole work is cohesive, flows logically step to step.

Following those directions is predominantly a mechanical task. Liken yourself to an artist creating a mosaic out of small, odd-shaped bits of colored stone. It is not enough to fit the pieces neatly together and cement them securely to the base. Any competent artisan could do that. The artistic test is whether the assembled bits form a picture that tells the story the artist has in mind. It is also essential that the artist have a story that has meaning for his audience. Artists deal in stone, paints, ceramics—any medium that meets their taste. Writers have only words at their disposal, and the quality of their work depends entirely on how they use their material. So, the editor's next task is to attend to these points:

1. Have unnecessary words been eliminated?
2. Are all thoughts clearly expressed and easily understood?
3. What about vague adjectives, too many adverbs?
4. Has gobbledygook been eliminated? What about businessese, clichés, slang, coarseness?
5. Is the writing stiff and stilted or too casual and folksy?
6. Is the writer's attitude friendly, courteous?

Once he has made necessary improvements, our editor is ready for his most important task. He rereads the entire work with four thoughts in mind:

1. Has the reader been given all the information he needs?
2. Has he been given answers to questions he might ask?
3. Has the report or letter fulfilled its purpose?
4. Does it read as if it has been written by a human being? (Frequently this is not the case.)

It is extremely helpful if the writer can put himself in the place of the reader and look at the work through that person's eyes. Knowing the idiosyncracies of the reader is important; does he demand details, does he want to know the source of every bit of information contained in the report? What are his likes and dislikes? Cater to his wishes; put him in a receptive frame of mind. He may be a bull, but you don't have to wave your red flannels at him.

Allowing a time interval between writing and editing is always advisable. Objectivity can be lost when one plunges directly from drafting to correcting written work. A few hours are better than none, but a good night's sleep before making revisions is much more desirable. And make no mistake about it, editing is equally as important as writing, and adequate attention should be given to it if the result is to be a credit to you. A careless editor can do more harm than good.

One other point must be made. Do not make final revisions on a draft that has been put through the wringer—words scratched out and replaced, sentences and paragraphs revised and repositioned. Type a fresh draft embodying all your changes and start over again. You will be surprised how differently the words read when they are easily decipherable. Also, you will spot grammatical and stylistic errors on a neatly typed sheet you would never have caught while working with a marked up draft.

The writer turned editor, when reading his work for the last time, should study the words he has written and ignore whatever else was in his mind when he wrote them. The reader has no crystal ball; he knows only what he sees. You, the writer, may know what you meant when you made a statement. The test is whether the words you wrote express your meaning accurately. Failure to meet this test is a principal cause of weakness in written reports.

That's about the best I can do on editing. To sum it up, I would suggest that when a writer turns himself into an editor of his own work, he should split himself into several individuals: his grammar school English teacher, his reader, a pragmatic businessman who can analyze the written word, and a person sensitive to the impression the attitude of the writer will have on the reader.

AN EXERCISE IN EDITING

An objective study of rules and principles is one thing; putting to work what one has learned is quite another, and the time has come for us to revise, correct, and edit the president's message in the annual report of Pin-Up Corporation.

This report is our introduction to a unique company, its colorful president and chief executive officer, Pevley Clip, and his brilliant young assistant, Charley Lightfoot, a Princeton educated descendant of famed Cherokee chieftains. Pin-Up, with headquarters in Shelbyville, Tennessee, is the largest manufacturer of clothespins in the south-central section of the state and has purveyed its wares successfully throughout the country for more than a hundred years. Pevley and his family own a controlling interest in the company, but the remainder of the stock is held by approximately two hundred individuals, and the president feels they are entitled to receive annually a complete and attractively printed report covering company operations. For several years Charley has written the message for his boss.

As soon as the books are closed, Charley gets a full set of financial statements from the comptroller, Eishade Waterhouse, and studies them carefully. He has already made himself familiar with other factors that have affected the results for the year just ended.

Charley knows Pevley Clip wants a short, snappy report. It must be straightforward but contain no explicit plans for the future since copies of the report will find their way to the hands of the competition, and Pevley is the last man in the world to give aid and comfort to the enemy.

Here is Charley's first draft:

To All Stockholders:

It is with the greatest pleasure that I report the 1982 results
to you. For the seventeenth consecutive year your company has
set new sales and profit records. Additionally, dividends were
increased for the fifteenth straight year. Our plants are running at
near capacity, and despite usual strong competition, our distribution channels are holding and in many areas increasing our share
of the market.

During the year just completed, we introduced two new
products. The first, a giant-size pin for the use in areas where
strong winds prevail, is selling better than projected in the
Virginias, Tennessee, North Carolina, and the Rocky Mountain
states. Results are disappointing in New England where the
necessary price increase has inhibited sales. Market strategies in
that area are being revalued.

The second innovation, a wooden pin with strong wire spring,
is doing well in test areas, and we will effect a rollout to the
entire East in the next six months.

The market for special orders remains firm, and this profitable
sideline will continue to be exploited to the fullest extent possible.

Financially your company is stronger than ever. Current ratio
is better than 2.4 to 1, and although short-term notes payable
have increased substantially in order to finance a much needed
inventory increase, it is expected that they will be all paid off on
or before June 30 of the current year.

One of the greatest strengths of your company is the high
morale of the many loyal employees in our plants and offices
throughout the country. More innovations will be marketed this
year, and we are confident in projecting even improved performance in 1983.

I offer my thanks to you for your continued support.

                              Pevley Clip
                              President

Charley studies what he has written, and the longer he looks at it, the less he likes it. This experience is not new; so, undaunted, he picks up his blue pencil and goes to work. The next two right-hand pages contain the notes Charley made when he reread the first draft, and the left-hand pages show what the message looked like after revisions and corrections.

To All Stockholders:

The year 1982 was an excellent one
~~It is with the greatest pleasure that I report~~
for your company. Sales and profits rose again
~~1982 results to you. For the seventeenth consecutive year~~
as they have every year since 1966.
~~your company has set new sales and profit records.~~ ~~Additionally,~~

at present
Dividends were increased for the fifteenth straight year. ∧ Our
close to   *sales,*
plants are running ∧ ~~at near~~ capacity and ∧ despite ~~usual strong~~
continue strong.
competition, ∧ ~~our distribution channels are holding and in~~

~~many areas increasing our share of the market.~~

During the year ~~just completed~~ we introduced ~~two~~

~~new products. The first,~~ a giant•size pin for use in areas
Sales are exceeding expectations
where ~~strong~~ winds prevail, ~~is selling better than projected~~
in all but one area.
~~in the Virginia, Tennessee, North Carolina and the Rocky~~

~~Mountain states. Sales are disappointing in New England~~

~~where the necessary price increase has inhibited sales.~~

~~Market strategies in that area are being reevalued.~~

⟵ ~~The second innovation,~~ A wooden pin with a strong
sold so   *that over* ⟵
wire spring ~~is doing~~ well in test areas ~~and~~ we will ~~effect~~
market it in
~~a roll out to~~ the entire east ∧ ~~in~~ *on part of the country.* (the next six months)

S
~~The market for~~ Special orders ~~remains firm and~~
are
~~this~~ ∧ profitable ~~side-line will continue to be exploited to~~

~~the fullest extent possible,~~ *and we will continue*
our efforts to expand this segment of our
business.

¶ 1.   Flowery. Not like Mr. Clips. Change. <u>Seventeenth</u> and <u>fifteenth</u> too much. Awkward — eliminate one. Change <u>at near</u> to <u>close to</u>. Delete unnecessary <u>usual</u>, <u>strong</u>. Distribution channels don't <u>hold</u> or <u>increase</u> anything. Rewrite. <u>Share of market</u> — too technical. Restructure whole ¶.

¶ 2 + 3.   Compress to single ¶. First sentence wordy — rewrite. Flush <u>geography</u> — rewrite <u>New England</u>. Why allude to failure there? Flush unnecessary words. <u>Strong</u> used twice — change. Change <u>roll-out</u>. Rewrite whole sentence.

¶ 4.   If special orders are profitable they aren't a <u>sideline</u>. Rewrite <u>exploited ...</u> <u>fullest extent possible</u>. Stilted — eliminate.

Financially your company is stronger than ever.
~~Current ratio is better than 2.4 to 1, and although~~ Short-
term notes payable have increased substantially in order
to finance a much needed inventory increase, ~~it is~~ but we expected
~~that~~ they will be ~~all~~ paid off, by the middle of the ~~on or before June 30 of the~~
current year.

One of the greatest strengths of your company is
the high morale of the ~~many loyal~~ employees in our plants
and offices throughout the country. To a large extent ~~More innovations will~~
our success can be attributed to their loyalty
~~be marketed this year and we are confident in projecting~~
and dedication to their responsibilities.
~~even improved performance in 1983~~

~~I offer my~~ Thanks ~~to~~ you for your continued support.

Tevley Clip
President

Our financial condition is excellent;
so is our competitive position. New
products have been developed and will
be introduced this year. Although the
national economy appears to be in
a recession with no firm indication
of a quick recovery and although inflation
poses a continuing threat to real prosperity,
nevertheless, we are confident that at the
end of this year we will again be
able to report record sales and earnings.

¶ 5.   First sentence OK – cheers!
How many stockholders recognize a current ratio? Those that are interested will work out the figure from the balance sheet that appears in the report. It is expected – weak – Flush. Eliminate unnessary words.

¶ 6.   Violates one point principle. Beef up compliment to employees.

¶ 7.   Add. Beat the drums. Get a new closing. I know we can do even better this year. Mr. Clip is positive we will. So, let's stick out our necks for 1983. At some time acknowledge unfavorable economic conditions.
Close – stilted – reword.

Charley has difficulty in deciphering his own handiwork so he dusts off his trusty Underwood and laboriously types out a clear copy of his revised message. He studies it carefully and makes a number of further corrections, the need for which had escaped him while he was working on the original draft. The next morning he checks the finished draft again before turning it over to a stenographer.

His labor is not yet finished; a further review is necessary to assure the typist was guilty of no misspellings, that punctuation is correct. He makes sure he has said what he wanted to say and that the message, as typed, is pleasing to the eye.

This is a copy of the message in its final form.

To All Stockholders:

The year 1982 was an excellent one for your company. Sales and profits rose again as they have every year since 1966. Dividends were increased for the fifteenth straight year. At present, plants are running close to capacity, and sales, despite competition, continue strong.

During the year we introduced a giant-size pin for use in areas where heavy winds prevail. Sales are exceeding expectations in all but one locality. A wooden pin with a strong wire spring sold so well in test areas that over the next six months we will market it in the entire eastern part of the country.

Special orders are profitable, and we will continue our efforts to expand this segment of our business.

Financially your company is stronger than ever. Short-term notes payable have increased substantially in order to finance a much needed inventory increase, but we expect they will be paid off by the middle of the current year.

One of the greatest strengths of our company is the high morale of the employees in our plants and offices throughout the country. To a large extent our success can be attributed to their loyalty and dedication to responsibilities.

Our financial condition is excellent; so is our competitive position. New products have been developed and will be introduced this year. Although the national economy appears to be in a recession with no firm indication of a quick recovery and although inflation poses a continuing threat to real prosperity, nevertheless, we are confident that at the end of this year we will again be able to report record sales and earnings.

Thank you for your continued support.

                                        Pevley Clip
                                        President

Charley likes the way the message reads—concise, smooth, and it sounds as if the old man had written it himself. He makes a copy for his file, sends the original to the boss, and decides there is time for a cup of coffee and a stroll through the plant before he tackles his next assignment. All is well with Charley and Pin-Up.

Do what Charley did and you'll make a competent writer and editor of yourself.

QUIZ

The following statements are related to what you have read in this chapter. What do they evoke in your mind? Space is available for your comments.

1. Time interval.

2. Grammar school English teacher, the reader, a pragmatic businessman, a person sensitive to the personality of the reader.

3. Clean draft.

4. Mosaic artist.

5. Information, answers, fulfillment of purpose, human authorship.

6. Reader has no crystal ball.

7. Check the typist.

8. Put yourself in reader's place.

9. First draft is final product—British Museum.

10. If you agree Charley did a good job, to what do you attribute his success?

No answers are supplied for this quiz. If you were uncertain in your replies, reread the chapter.

4

How's this for starters?

> Dere sir
>
> Inclosed is $4 Plese
> send ~~you~~ yore book
> beter riting to Sam'l Johnson
>   R F D 1
>   Frog Hollow
>   W. Va 89706
>
>   Singed
>   Sam'l Johnson

I have been spending an unconscionable amount of time reading what the competition has to say about letter writing. All the experts talk about starting with a good quality white paper measuring 8½ by 11 inches, go on through heading, inside address, salutation, body, complimentary (whatever that connotes) close, and signature. Strangely enough, not one mentions that every letter should be dated. The reader is told what size envelope he should use, how to fold the sheet of good quality white paper, and that a stamp of the proper denomination should be affixed to the upper right-hand corner of the envelope or the mailman won't deliver the letter. A number of experts mention Block or

Modified Block style. I finally figured out what that means, but I'm keeping quiet about it because I don't want to confuse you.

According to the experts Sam'l Johnson should be shipped back to the bush leagues forthwith. His letter was written on a sheet of lined greenish paper torn from a pad; he ignored such vital items as inside address and complimentary close. His spelling is atrocious, his punctuation nonexistent, and he wrote with a stubby pencil instead of an electric typewriter.

Yet, I'll bet you dollars to donuts Sam'l got *beter riting* by return mail. His letter lacked no important element; the $4 was enclosed, he stated what he wanted and gave instructions where to send the book. Everything else is a mere detail.

We aren't all Sam'l Johnsons, and we should attempt to follow a standard format when writing business letters. The point I am trying to make is that what is in the letter is the important factor. Letters should present a pleasing appearance to assure a favorable reception by the reader, but I am not going to spend my time or waste yours on a discussion of whether you should or should not indent paragraphs. Let your secretary, who has attended an excellent business school, instruct you in such niceties.

What I will discuss briefly are a few of the principles governing the art of business letter writing.

WRITING STYLE

Why do executives write business letters? Let's consider that for a moment or two. We write because we have something to say: giving or asking for information or making a request for a decision or action. Buying, selling, complaining, or answering complaints—you name it, letters are written about it.

But why write a letter? Why not a phone call or a three martini lunch, provided a nondrinking junior is along to remember what was said or decided? Basically, it is a matter of logistics. You can lunch with only one group a day, and it becomes inconvenient if you are in Boston and your lunchmate is in San Diego. Then too, no one keeps minutes of a luncheon meeting, and six months later who remembers anything except that the Newcastle Potted Salmon hors d'oeuvre was overspiced with mace and cloves.

The telephone is a wonderful instrument, and dividends paid by Ma Bell have kept the wolf from the door of countless widows and orphans. But a phone call, like lunches, leaves no permanent record behind it. In addition, at times it is advisable for several people to know about agreements made in a phone conversation, and this makes a memo necessary. Also, one individual's understanding of what was decided in a phone conversation might not concur with the other person's conclusion from the same discussion.

Many business letters are written because writers need a record of the matters discussed in them. They should be written clearly so there will be no misunderstanding of the message. They should be concise and as short as possible.

Individuals who have no problem in talking over the phone or face to face with people often freeze when they write a letter. When that happens, the letter might begin like this: "In answer to your recent request I wish to advise that . . ." How do you prevent such a debacle? Simple. Imagine you are talking to the other person instead of writing to him. Tell him what you want to say in natural conversational English. Don't try to jazz up your writing so it becomes a formal, stilted treatise. To me, natural conversational English contains no coarseness, no jargon, and is grammatically and syntactically sound.

You would never think of opening a conversation with the sentence fragment quoted above. Read your letter aloud. How does it strike your ear? If you cringe when you hear what you have written, try it again.

Be natural, be clear, be concise.

ATTITUDE

Be positive. Plunge in and tell it like it is. At the same time be polite, pleasant. Use active, not passive voice. (Twenty-two words that contain five suggestions. Succinct but not abrasive.)

Never be insensitive to the attitude and position of your reader. Try to see things from his point of view—answer his questions, show you have an understanding of his side of the matter. Don't stampede him.

Let us take a minute or two to think about the personality of words. When we talk face to face with someone, the words we use carry only a portion of the burden of communication. Facial expressions, gestures, inflections play an important role in transmitting our message. Remember Owen Wister's Virginian's warning, "When you say that, smile." We can see a smile, but we can't hear it over a telephone or detect it in a page of typescript. In writing, words carry the whole load. A friendly jibe in conversation may become an insult in writing as the reader cannot see the grin or catch the tone of voice that accompanied the crack.

So, be careful how you express yourself in writing. Read the words you have written from the reader's point of view. Avoid sarcasm; don't be cute. Adopt a friendly yet dignified, courteous style.

SUBJECT

It seems to me that it is only common sense to show the subject of a letter in the middle of the sheet directly above the *Dear Sir*. Underlining draws attention to it.

Subject: <u>Lease on Fifth Avenue Store</u>

Dear Sir:

The reader is prepared for what he will be reading, and perhaps the person who opens the mail might be motivated to attach the file to the letter before putting it on the boss's desk. Showing the subject is another way to make it easy for the reader and put him into a receptive frame of mind.

I have developed a great time-saver in handling personal business correspondence. If I receive a request for information from my insurance broker, I type my reply in a blank area of his letter, make a copy at the office, paying my dime, of course, return the original to the broker, and retain the copy for my file. Request and reply on the same piece of paper—unheard of. Businesses can't run that way, I suppose, but individuals can. On second thought, why shouldn't businesses handle at least part of their correspondence in such a manner? Unfortunately, I am unable to patent the process.

Believe it or not, but a few days ago I found myself in the middle of a sometimes acrimonious dispute whether *Subject* should appear above or below *Dear Sir*. The dispute was settled with a decision worthy of Solomon. If the writer preferred to list the subject above the salutation, he should do so, and should he wish to place it below, that was equally his perogative.

In other words, put the subject anywhere you please so long as you show it somewhere.

DEAR SIR:, DEAR MADAM:, GENTLEMEN:, TO WHOM IT MAY CONCERN:

Rule number one is: If you know the name of the person to whom you are writing, address him by name. Make your letter as personal as possible.

If you are writing to the unknown purchasing agent of a corporation, you should refer to him as *Dear Sir*. To call an individual *Gentlemen* would be inappropriate. Use *Gentlemen* when you are not directing your letter to any individual in an organization.

What do you do when a young friend who is job hunting asks you for a general recommendation? To start your letter *To Whom It May Concern* sounds awfully stilted. If you write *Dear Sir* and the personnel director happens to be a woman, your friend might not be treated with the warmth he deserves. Why not try *Dear Sir or Madam*?

At times the chairman of a corporation sends a letter to four hundred thousand stockholders and starts it *Dear Stockholders*. That sounds phony to me. I would much rather see the letter headed *To All Stockholders*.

Executives who are personal friends may use first names in correspondence provided the full name of the addressee appears in the address shown at the top of the letter and on the envelope. There is nothing wrong with starting a business letter *Dear George* and signing it with your given name. First names would not be used, however, if the letter involves legal matters or policy at a high level. In such cases a full signature is recommended.

CONTENT

Why are you writing the letter? You should have a reason, and if you state it in the subject, your reader will at least know what you are writing about.

What points do you wish to make? They should be set forth in the first paragraph. Why beat around the bush? You are a busy man (we hope), and so is the person who will read your letter. Make your points clearly and tactfully, and if your letter calls for answers, be sure to state exactly what you want to know. Don't leave it to the addressee to figure out what information or decision you expect from him.

In taking such an approach a writer must be careful not to give an impression of Napoleonic arrogance. That is where tact comes in. It is possible to be direct without bulling about like an enraged African buffalo.

If you are a friend of the person to whom you are writing, don't start your letter with a reference to your Sunday golf game or Saturday's drunken brawl. Business letters should confine themselves to business matters. If you feel you should add a personal note, write it in your own hand at the bottom of the sheet.

Which brings up a different type of business letter. Let us say the bank you do business with sponsors an event on the PGA tour, and you were invited to play in the Pro-Am the day before the start of the tournament proper. To your delight you were paired with Tom Watson, and you enjoyed the experience thoroughly. Your thank-you note to the bank officer responsible for your invitation is really a business communication, but it lists no subject, starts with *Dear Bill* and is written in an informal and personal vein. No strictly business matters should be tacked on to that letter.

Don't mix business and social matters. Keep them distinctly apart.

SIGN YOUR MAIL YOURSELF

Not long ago a company in which I owned what I considered to be a substantial block of stock was purchased by a conglomerate at an exceptionally generous price. My profits were large, and with a feeling of sincere gratitude, I wrote the company president to compliment him on how well he had run the company and to thank him for his part in making my profits as large as they were. It was a damn good letter. Ten days later I received a reply, equally well written, friendly, appreciative, but beneath the signature, which was a model of penmanship with each letter clearly decipherable, appeared the initials S. P. The president had been too busy to sign his mail and had delegated that function to his secretary. Perhaps she had even composed the letter as well as signed it.

I am still grateful for the money the president made for me, but a stroke of his secretary's pen took all the pleasure out of the correspondence.

Situations may arise that prevent an executive from signing his mail. An unexpected trip, a sudden illness—these are legitimate excuses, but they can be handled without damage to the feelings of the recipient of the letter. The secretary types a note at the bottom of the page: "Mr. Blank, after dictating this letter, was unexpectedly called away but asked that I send it to you immediately." The initials L. S. appear under the boss's name and after the note.

When I receive the letter, I smile. Blank is a great guy—he's really concerned about me, and L. S., whoever she is, knows how to make a fellow feel good. The whole deal didn't take a minute, but what a difference it made.

So, sign your mail or explain why you don't. If you are too damn important to sign missives directed to such as I, malediction on you.

THE CLOSE

How do you wind up a letter? In the old days it was not at all unusual to find at the bottom of the last page something like this:

Hoping this finds you as it leaves me,

> Your obedient servant,
> *Thadeus Pinfeather*

At least he didn't write *Hopefully,* but by modern standards, spelling his name properly was the only thing he didn't do wrong. Let's look at what Thadeus would have written were he living in our day.

Actually there are two closes to every letter. The first is the windup of the message, and the second is what is called the complimentary close.

When you have finished what you have to say, stop. Don't ramble on about the weather, the travails of your favorite ball team, or even the recent gyrations of the Dow Jones average. This advice refers solely to a business communication; it is possible that the recent hot spell, the doings of the Dodgers, or the price of General Motors might be part of your message in a personal letter to a friend. There, the situation is different but business correspondence should confine itself strictly to business matters.

Now, let's consider the few words above your signature. Should you write, *Yours truly, Yours very truly, Very truly yours, Sincerely,* or even *Cordially?* I suppose it's a matter of habit and personal preference. Appropriateness also must be considered. Not one of the closes mentioned is unconventional. The first three are more formal than the last two. Actually, all are trite. I doubt that anyone who reads a letter and scans the close ever stops to consider what the words mean. When you write *Yours truly* are you telling the addressee that you really belong to him, honest you do? I very much doubt it.

Personally, I prefer *Yours truly.* The adverb *very* adds little as a modifier of *truly.* The simpler, the better. Thus, if a person to whom I am writing is a stranger to me, I close with *Yours truly.* If I know him or her or have developed a relationship through lengthy correspondence. I would probably end with the more personal *Sincerely.* To me, *Cordially* connotes an even closer friendly relationship.

If the individual is well known to me in a social or business sense, I would probably close with *Regards* or *Best wishes* and would sign my first name instead of initials and surname.

In summary, sign off as you will, but let your close be appropriate and in keeping with the circumstances.

Personal letters are another matter entirely, and on them you can sign off in any way that suits your pleasure. I am told that an elderly Lothario, when sending a note and a final check to a mistress he was in the process of replacing, habitually closed his farewell in this manner:

With my best wishes to you and your lawyer.

COPIES OF BUSINESS LETTERS AND MEMORANDUMS

On letters, the names of the persons to whom copies are being sent are listed below the initials of the writer and typist at the lower left-hand corner of the letter.

WGR/EVE
cc.   J. P. Jones
     S. F. Decatur
Encl.

If other material is being sent along with the letter the abbreviation *Encl.*, for enclosure, is typed below the initials or names as shown above.

On an interoffice memo the practice is different in that the names of the persons to whom copies are being sent appear at the top of the sheet.

   To: Ely Culbertson
From: P. H. Sims
  cc.   S. Lentz
      W. Work

In the example, Culbertson is the man who is responsible for handling whatever it is that Sims is writing about. Lentz and Work are given copies to keep them informed of the situation. Should they be involved in handling the matter their names would appear with Culbertson's as corecipients of the memo.

The rule of thumb is: If an individual is being given responsibility in a matter he should be made a corecipient of a memo; if not, he should merely receive a copy.

I shall close this chapter with a final exhibition of petulance. I can't abide people who, when sending a memo to three or four individuals, write their initials next to their name on the original and allow the copy machine to reproduce them on all copies. True, this action may save five or ten seconds of their valuable time, but what would they do with the saving?

Reproduced initials are cold, unfriendly, even. The more important an executive is, the more aware he should be of the feelings of his juniors. I would be much happier if Sims wrote his name at the bottom of a memo he sent me or even signed off *Hal*.

A case can be made for reproduced initials or signature when the list of recipients is a long one.

QUIZ

Space is provided for your answers to this test.

1. Sam'l Johnson's letter, despite its shortcomings, did fulfill several of the requirements of a good letter. What were they?

2. What is the best way to discover if your letter writing style is stilted?

3. Letters have advantages and disadvantages when compared with phone calls and meetings. What are some of them?

4. The statement was made that every letter has two closes. What points was the author trying to make?

5. Demonstrate you understand the theory and form with respect to copies of letters and memos.

ANSWERS

1. *a.* Money was enclosed.
   b. He stated what he wanted.
   c. He gave instructions where to send the book.
2. Read aloud what you have written. If you write as you would talk (when you are on your best behavior) your language will not sound stilted. If the words sound awkward to you, rephrase.

3. Advantage of letters:
   a. They leave a tangible record in at least two files.
   b. Meetings are, at times, difficult to arrange.
   c. Conference phone calls can be difficult or impossible to organize, but copies of letters can be sent to all interested parties.

   Disadvantages of letters:
   a. People often do not express themselves as clearly in writing as they do in speaking.
   b. When you write a letter you are aware only of your own feelings. The attitude and receptiveness of the addressee are unknown to you, which is not the case when you talk face to face with him.
   c. Confusion and misunderstandings can be clarified during a conversation but necessitate further correspondence when they stem from unclear written communication.

4. a. The first close in a business communication is the windup of the message. When you have made your last point, stop. Don't ramble on.
   b. The second, or complimentary close, should be a matter of personal taste but should be appropriate and in keeping with the circumstances.
   c. The close of a personal letter relies entirely on the preference of the writer.

5. On letters, copies are shown at the lower left-hand corner of the sheet, under the initials of the writer and typist, followed by *Encl.* if enclosures are attached. On memos, copies are sent to all interested parties. If anyone, in addition to the addressee is responsible for doing something, he should be listed as a coaddressee rather than as a recipient of a copy.

   Memo copies are listed in this fashion:

   To: _____
   From: _____
   cc.   _____
            _____
            _____

BUSINESS REPORTS

5

A few million men and women write thousands of millions of words each year and brazenly call them business reports. If all the copies of these reports were stacked in a pile it would possibly girdle the globe twelve times at the equator or comfortably reach the moon. The paper staircase probably cost more to produce than the technology developed to put men on the moon if we include in expense not only writing time but also the reading time of the poor souls who must slog through the verbiage.

If a way could be found to cut reading volume by 25 percent, industry would save tens of millions of dollars a year. During my years of experience in business and teaching I have read thousands of reports and of that number all but a handful would have been improved immeasurably by reducing the length by a least a quarter, provided the authors knew the art of organization and presentation.

Another factor is involved here. The vast majority of individuals does not relish the obligation to produce a report. When given a writing assignment, how many of us honestly enjoy the opportunity to display our literary talents? Isn't the more common response, "Damn, what a bummer!" Writing is hard work and all of us realize it. What some of us don't realize is that the ability to produce clear, concise, and convincing prose is an asset that can greatly impress our bosses and improve our chances to climb the ladder to success in our organization.

There is no reason to be apprehensive about a report writing assignment. It is an involved procedure, true, but there are guidelines that can be followed, basic rules that can be mastered, tricks of the trade that can be learned. The earlier pages of this book contain fundamental information on choice and usage of words, grammer, syntax, attitude, development of an attractive style, advice on editing, and so forth.

In this chapter I'll get into the actual production of a report and the steps that must be taken before the writer picks up his pencil and starts the first draft. I'll also discuss exhibits and how to avoid mistakes that weaken a report.

AUDIENCE, ROLE, ASSIGNMENT

The first obligation of a person asked to write a report is to relate the three words written above to the project.

To whom will the report be addressed, what other individuals will read it? How familiar are they with the subject? What positions do they enjoy in the company hierarchy? Are you aware of any personal prejudices of members of the audience with regard to the subject? Knowing the answers to some or all of these questions should influence the attitude of the writer.

He should also consider his role. Is he an acknowledged expert in the area? Is he informing or instructing, or is his purpose to convince his audience to approve his recommendations? What should his attitude be?

Analysis of the assignment is closely connected with role study. Precisely what is the writer asked to do? What issues are germane to the subject; what are irrelevant? What is the scope of the assignment? Is the report to be expository, persuasive, or a mixture of both?

I hope you can see the necessity of clarification of these points before writing a report. As you read the remainder of this chapter it will be made evident to you how audience, role, and assignment are always in the mind of an experienced report writer.

TYPES OF REPORTS

Reports fit into one of two categories: action reports or expository reports.

The purpose of the action report is to inform, analyze, draw conclusions, and, most importantly, to recommend convincingly a specific course of action. On the other hand, an expository report merely sets forth the information and facts germane to an issue but makes no attempt to draw conclusions or propose action. By its nature an action report should be persuasive; an expository report should be coldly clinical with no attempt made to sway opinion.

The primary function of management is to make decisions and, based on them, to establish strategies designed to achieve chosen objectives. In our present society no executive of even a moderately large organization can be expected to know everything that is going on in his area of responsibility. Thus, he must rely to a considerable extent on reports submitted to him by his staff and his operating superintendents if his ultimate decisions are to be of the highest quality. Information given him as well as recommendations made to him must therefore be accurate and comprehensive; conclusions must be sound, realistic, and convincingly presented. Above all, recommendations should develop logically from the evidence on which they are based and be consistent with the situation as it exists rather than relate to the situation as it ought to be. In short, recommendations must be practical.

STEPS IN DEVELOPING A REPORT

No single established format has been agreed on for business reports. Every executive and organization sets ground rules covering the form a report should follow. Juniors must learn to adapt themselves to the idiosyncrasies and prejudices of bosses. If form is a constant variable, development of content is not.

The vast majority of action reports involves the following elements:

1. Collection and organization of material.
2. Analysis of the material.
3. Conclusions and recommendations based on the analysis.
4. Development of a specific course of action.

Each of these segments is important enough to deserve a few paragraphs.

Collection of material.   When the big boss calls Charley to his office Monday morning and bellows, "Charley, what the hell's the matter with profits in the Three I territory last month?" the first thing Charley doesn't do is retort, "How the hell do I know?" One does not address Pevley Clip, president and chief executive officer of Pin-Up Corporation, in such a manner if one enjoys his job and has aspirations to hold it a while longer.

Charley, with a sure instinct for self-preservation, tugs at his forelock and answers, "I'll find out and let you know."

"Do that," growls Clip, "and don't forget your recommendations. A week from today will be fine." A peremptory gesture dismisses Charley, and Clip returns to his study of the report that is engaging his attention at the moment.

Charley returns to his office and begins to think. His first job will be to secure a copy of the report that disclosed the dismal showing of the Iowa, Illinois, and Indiana division. He'll get that from Baynes Scattergood, general sales manager, who won't have any answers but will be smart enough to know he can't stonewall Clip's number one assistant. The next stop will be the Treasury Department. The Three I territory is a profit center, and a study of financial records will give Charley a clue as to how bad the situation really is. Eishade Waterhouse, the comptroller, will do all he can to satisfy Charley. He suffers from an inferiority complex, is mortally afraid of Clip, and will welcome an opportunity to do a favor for the agent of the old man.

Charley's mind is now hitting on all four. He'll call the division manager in Terre Haute, pick his brains, and secure permission from him to visit managers of the three or four hardest hit branches. Charley counts on his fingers, a habit he has never been able to break: Monday and Tuesday at the home office here in Shelbyville, three days in the field, the weekend at home organizing and writing the report—that gives him Monday morning for typing, editing, and putting the report in final shape. "Hell," he says to himself. "It's a cinch."

Charley may be young; self-confidence is his forte, and modesty is a characteristic foreign to his nature, but he is smart enough to know that only a fool tries to do anything strictly on his own. When he needs information, Charley pumps dry every source open to him, turns over all the rocks he can find, and ferrets around until he knows everything that is to be known on a subject.

Analysis of material. Back in Shelbyville, Charley starts to work on his analysis Saturday morning. All the information he has collected has been assembled under various headings. Among them are: manufacturing costs, marketing expense, unit sales, gross volume, competition, and general economic conditions. The answer, he is sure, will be found in one or more of these areas.

Manufacturing costs are well within budget—no problem there. Also, he notes no perceptible change in the economic environment; so those two elements can be, to a large extent, disregarded. Both will be dismissed in a sentence or two in his report. Why waste time flogging a dead horse?

Unit sales are spotty. They are down substantially in Iowa, up slightly in Illinois, and much higher in Indiana. Illinois shows a mixed pattern. The western part of the state had a serious drop, but sales around Chicago and the eastern part of the state were up. Charley gets a map of the Three I territory and color codes the performance of all the branches in the three states. The map will be an exhibit attached to his report. The sales pattern looks fishy.

Gross volume supplies a further clue. Revenues are way down in Iowa, weak in Illinois, and barely steady in Indiana despite the increase in unit sales.

Marketing expenses, higher across the board, supply another clue. Advertising has jumped dramatically in the whole territory; so have discounts given to distributors. The departure from normal in this account aroused Charley's suspicions as soon as he spotted it. Why such an increase?

Competition supplied the answer. On the first of the previous month, a mammoth mail-order house had cut the price on its competing clothespin, but, Charley had discovered, the reduction was limited to Iowa and a few contiguous counties in western Illinois. Other manufacturers, Pin-Up included, had met the price cut, and Pin-Up had also increased advertising allocations considerably in an attempt to maintain market share.

All right, but why increase advertising and cut prices in Illinois and Indiana where Pin-Up was encountering no unusual competitive pressure? Lash Monger, Three I division manager, had blown it. Meeting price competition in Iowa and a few counties in Illinois could possibly be defended, perhaps even increasing advertising, but what was the sense of extending the changes to the rest of the territory?

Charley worked on his analysis until he was confident he had covered every relevant issue. He then turned his attention to organizing the conclusions he had developed from his analysis.

Conclusions and recommendations. What alternative courses of action were available to Pin-Up? What other problems might ensue if the various strategies were adopted?

For instance, if special discounts to distributors in Indiana were discontinued at once, what would be the effect on sales for the next month or two? Charley had been around long enough to know that every action is accompanied by an equal and opposite reaction, and measurement of possible reaction was a must before any change in operation was made. He thought through the advantages and disadvantages of each of the strategies he had outlined and finally settled on the one that in his judgment had the best chance of extricating the division from the position it was in.

Course of action. Sunday morning Charley wrestled with remedial action and in the afternoon made his decision and wrote out the course of action he would recommend to Pevley Clip. The plan was set forth in detail. Who should do what was stated, when he should do it, and why it should be done was laid out in one, two, three, order so there could be no uncertainty on the part of anyone.

The evening was devoted to writing, editing, and rewriting the report. It would run to three typed pages plus two exhibits, and the draft would be ready for him before ten o'clock Monday, allowing time for last minute improvements before the finished report would be typed, checked for typographical errors, and submitted to the boss by noon.

WRITING THE REPORT

Let us take a closer look at the steps Charley took as he prepared to write his report and how he handled the actual writing.

First, precisely what was his assignment? He wrote down Clip's exact words. "What the hell's the matter with profits in the Three I territory last month?" The scrap of paper was never out of sight or mind while Charley worked on the project. He knew from bitter experience that nothing must divert him from his primary objective—fulfilling his instructions. During his investigations he might discover that the manager of the Des Moines office had embezzled $80,000 of the company funds and the warehouse in Des Plaines contained, in addition to a few million clothespins, a cache of nine tons of marijuana. Both of these bits of information were important enough to be reported to the boss but were subjects not to be included in his present assignment unless they were factors in the profit decline in the Three I territory.

Charley also kept the lowering visage of Pevley Clip constantly in his mind. He knew his boss's likes and dislikes as well as knew those of his own wife. Clip couldn't abide rash assumptions—everything reported to him must be supported by evidence or reasoned conclusions. No one could con Pevley, and those who tried did so at the risk of instant dismissal. In addition, like others with Napoleonic complexes, Clip tolerated no familiarity from his underlings. Elephantine humor was his perogative alone; he freely ignored the rules of syntax and grammar in his speech but tolerated no slips by members of his staff. Profanity and slang in the mouths of others was an anathema to him, but his own speech was liberally dotted with "damns" and "hells." Clip was living proof of the validity of the theory of atavism; he was a spiritual and perhaps a lineal descendant of Genghis Khan, Attila the Hun, and Billy the Kid. Why did Charley work for him? For that matter why did anyone work for him? Charley had the answer. Clip was intensely loyal to those who played the game by his rules and predictable standards, and he rewarded them handsomely. He was a man from whom you could learn. Then, too, he was capable of unexpected acts of generosity. The previous winter Charley's wife had suffered a serious illness, and one morning shortly after her discharge from the hospital, Charley received a note from Clip ordering him to take her on a Caribbean cruise and enclosing a personal check that would more than cover all expenses.

Life around Pevley Clip wasn't a bed of roses, but it had its compensations. It is understandable why Charley was never unmindful of the personality of the man he was writing to.

Outline.   Charley did not feel that making an outline of what his report would cover was beneath his dignity, and he went about its preparation exactly as he had been taught to do in sixth grade. He had learned that a detailed outline performed several important functions that aided him when he wrote a report.

When properly prepared, an outline assured a logical progression to the report. Points would follow in orderly sequence, and there would be no jumping about when he started to write. If the outline was followed rigidly—an essential requirement—it would eliminate the possibility of allowing himself to be trapped into irrelevant digressions. The outline would make it impossible to forget or ignore important issues once writing was under way. Finally, and by no means least importantly, the outline would supply the headings for each section of the report.

Knowing all this, Charley worked on his outline until he was satisfied it met his standards.

First draft.   The next step was to flesh out the outline. The writing came surprisingly easy since he already had a framework for what he wanted to say. Charley was a fast writer and a wordy one, but this weakness did not worry him as he never considered the first draft to be even close to the finished product.

Editing.   Charley did his writing on lined yellow sheets of paper he kept in a three-ring binder. He wrote only on the right-hand page, making minor corrections on the text itself, and using the left-hand page for major revisions. When the first draft had been carefully edited, a second draft was written, embodying all the changes made. Editing and rewriting continued until Charley was satisfied with the result.

Final draft.   When the report was typed, Charley went over it still again as he had learned that weaknesses had a habit of showing up more clearly in type than in his crabbed handwriting. Once final corrections were made, the report received its final typing, and Charley checked it carefully once more to catch typographical errors and to make sure his figures were correctly copied.

At long last the report was ready for the eagle eyes of Pevley Clip.

GENERAL SUGGESTIONS ON REPORT WRITING

The quality of recommendations made is of paramount importance and so is the specificity with which a course of action is set forth. Clear thinking is essential in writing a convincing report, and nothing can take the place of being right. Yet, many otherwise excellent reports are inferior to what they ought to be because the writer goes astray in one or more areas.

THE START

Reports should begin this way:

                                                                Date:

To:
From:
Subject:

(Note: *To* always comes before *From*.)

Starting in this fashion is neither difficult nor intellectually demanding, but it is important. Problems start to pile up when the writer begins his first sentence. He will do well if he emulates Caesar who, as I recall from my brief study of him, was in the habit of plunging *in medias res*. His example is an excellent one. Don't start by describing the creation of the earth and continue to the present, eon by eon. Don't spend a page or two warming up the motor. As the tennis players and golfers do, a writer should ready himself before the match begins, and when the bell rings, he should be off and running. (An excellent example of mixed metaphors.)

Should Charley be asked to develop a price for a new product, an excellent beginning for his report would be: "I recommend a price of $12.85 each for silver-plated clothespins." Pevley Clip would respond favorably to such a beginning. He is given the recommendation immediately, and as he reads the report, he can test the analysis against the recommended price to see whether the argument is always consistent. On the other hand, if the price is withheld until the final paragraph, it is much more difficult for the reader to follow the trend of the analysis.

A report is not like a detective story in which the perpetrator of the dastardly deed is not unveiled until the final chapter when each of the clues is tied into the denouement by the brilliant deductions of the sleuth. Neither is it a cliff-hanger in which the intrepid heroine plummets from crisis to crisis with monumental aplomb and an immaculate coiffure. There should be no dramatics in a report, no sudden revelations, no surprises.

Many executives, especially if a report is a long one, require that a half-page synopsis of the conclusions and recommendations be attached to the front of the report. This practice is particularly helpful when the problem is a complex one and the answer is not as simple as setting a price on a silver-plated clothespin.

Putting the recommendations up front is a good way for a writer to make it easy for his reader to follow and understand his argument.

USE OF INFORMATION

Across the nation rolls the report writer's plaintive wail, "I can't get enough information." At times this concern is real, and we'll get to it later, but far more problems are caused by a plethora of information than by a dearth of that commodity. Writers of reports at times feel an unquenchable urge to tell everything they know when they grip a no. 2 pencil and start writing. This tendency is aggravated if the boss is one of those benign souls who does not believe in stifling the creative and imaginative impulses of his assistant and neglects to impose a strict length limit on the report he has commissioned. It should be a matter of great interest to a reader to know that Sebastião José de Carvalho e melo, Marques do Pombal, 1699–1782, Portuguese statesman, expelled the Jesuits, curbed the Inquisition, reformed the schools, built up Brazil, and reconstructed Lisbon after the 1755 earthquake. Yet, what have these gems of information got to do with a marketing plan for Pin-Up's introduction of a new 4½-inch clothespin?

Researching a report unearths much more information than a concise, well-written report can use. The writer's problem is what material to use and what to discard. Generally speaking, information germane to the issues being analyzed should be mentioned in a report. Data should be used to make sure a reader will have a sufficient background to understand a situation. It is also employed to support analysis and conclusions. All other information is redundant.

ASSUMPTIONS

There is a vast distinction between a fact and an unsupported assumption, and a writer, if he is to earn the credibility of his reader, must clearly label his assumptions as assumptions and not try to pass them off as facts. It is essential to establish the validity and reasonableness of assumptions as fully as possible. Vehemence of language cannot overcome shallowness of argument. When a writer starts a sentence, "I am absolutely convinced that . . ." the reader usually suspects he is being conned. On the other hand if a writer makes an assumption and supports it with factual evidence and if the assumption then appears realistic, the reader can accept it not as a fact but as a reasonable probability. Many reports are unacceptably weak because of faulty and invalid assumptions.

FICTION WRITING

We are told that necessity is the mother of invention, and a review of the history of industrial production tends to support this adage. Invention, however, is not in the purview of the report writer. If a piece of evidence is missing, he cannot manufacture it. He cannot embroider on the truth. Imaginative approaches are to be applauded, but imagination and fabrication are not interchangeable qualities. Stay with the information you have or can secure, but don't substitute fiction for fact.

NOT ENOUGH INFORMATION

No one has ever had all the information he thinks he needs, and if the past is a valid indicator of the future, no one ever will. When the writer is confronted with a blank spot during research of an issue, he should ask himself why the missing information is necessary. Not infrequently, further study will result in the discovery that the information isn't as indispensable as it first appeared to be, but if it still seems required, he should ask himself how it could be obtained. What would be the cost in time and money to secure it? If the information were obtained, what could it show and what would be done dependent on what the information disclosed? It would then be necessary to make a decision whether or not to expend the time and money to locate the missing link. It is not adequate to take the attitude that since the information is not available, a writer may ignore what might be an important area.

QUIZ

Space is provided for your answers.
1. Contrast expository and action reports.

2. What are the four steps a writer goes through in writing an action report?

3. Outlines. A few words on this subject, please.

4. What mental process do you go through if there is an information gap?

5. Assumptions. A sentence or two on this subject, if you will.

ANSWERS

1. Action reports inform, analyze, draw conclusions, and recommend a course of action.
   Expository reports set forth information and facts on the issues involved but make no attempt to draw conclusions or propose action.
   Action reports are persuasive, expository ones are coldly clinical.

2. *a.* Collection and organization of material.
    b. Analysis of material.
    c. Conclusions and recommendations based on analysis.
    d. Development of specific course of action.
3. A properly prepared outline:
    a. Assures logical progression in a report.
    b. Eliminates danger of irrelevant digressions.
    c. Removes possibility of forgetting important issues.
    d. Supplies headings for each section of a report.
4. *a.* Determine that information is actually vital.
    b. Determine cost and time expenditure to secure it.
    c. Determine if cost is worthwhile.
5. Assumptions must always be labeled as such. Under no circumstances regard them as facts. The more evidence that can be supplied to support them, the greater the chance to move them from vague possibilities closer to probabilities. But no matter how strongly supported, they are still assumptions, not facts.

EXHIBITS

The purpose of exhibits is to explain, clarify, support, and supplement the text of a report. Important facts disclosed by an exhibit should be stated in the text, which must stand independent of exhibits, so that it is not necessary to check exhibits for information developed in them but left hidden there and not mentioned in the text.

Exhibits, too, must be able to stand on their own and not require explanation in the text for full understanding. They should have proper headings, be complete, clear, and easily understandable should a reader study them before he reads the text of a report. Appending explanatory notes to exhibits so a reader can follow the methodology of their development is not only proper but desirable. To explain in the text how an exhibit is constructed is improper. Exhibits present facts and figures but no conclusions. These are reported only in the text.

Exhibits must provide the source of figures used in the report itself. Thus, if the text states, "Exhibit IV shows that fixed costs are $185,347," the exhibit should contain an itemized list of costs totaling that amount. The reader should not be forced to pick from the maze of figures in Exhibit IV a combination that reaches the desired total.

Executives are usually familiar with a number of different kinds of exhibits, and the skilled writer may use a variety of them in his reports. He will be expected to employ some or all of these types of exhibits.

1. Figures. Balance sheets, profit and loss statements, and so on. Many more figures can be shown on a report exhibit than should be included on a visual aid used in a presentation. It is not unusual to see five- to ten-year comparative financial statements on a single sheet. The only restriction on the amount of numbers is that they should not be too small for the eyes of myopic elderly directors. (See Exhibit I.)

2. Line graphs. Exhibit II is an illustration of this type of graph, which is an excellent means of showing progression of performance from period to period in a few selected accounts. Note that each line is clearly identified and the lines themselves are differentiated so that, should they happen to cross, there will be no confusion as to which is which. Line differentiation is superior to color coding if it is necessary to make several copies of the exhibit and the copy equipment does not reproduce in color.

Line graphs are not as precise as columns of figures. A study of Exhibit II reveals that profits in the most recent year were slightly over $9 million and dividends were approximately $4.7 million. To enter the precise amounts for each year on the graph would congest it to such an extent its value would be lost. The same would be true if retained earnings, income taxes paid, and research and development costs were charted on the same graph.

3. Bar graphs.   Exhibit III is a simple example of a bar graph. It shows only gross sales, is uncluttered and easy to understand. In this instance vertical bars are used. They can also be drawn horizontally. A report might refer to this graph thusly: "Exhibit III shows that sales have increased sevenfold between the first and last years." You will note that the vertical axis (dollar volume) starts at zero and that the bars are of equal width.

Exhibit IV is totally unacceptable as it contains two serious and deceptive flaws. The information it conveys should be identical with that contained in the last half of Exhibit III, but the impression on the viewer is entirely different. Part of this deception is caused by the vertical axis (dollar volume) starting at $50 million instead of zero. The increase in sales from about $56 million to $80 million is 43 percent, a handsome rise, to be sure, but it appears to be a great deal more than that in the graph. Also, the final bar is four times as wide as the first

EXHIBIT I
PIN-UP CORPORATION
Balance sheets
($000)

	12/31/xx	12/31/xx	12/31/xx	12/31/xx	12/31/xx
Assets					
Cash	$ 73	$ 71	$ 346	$ 140	$ 94
Accounts receivable	246	336	221	217	282
Inventories and prepaid expenses	1,104	675	558	652	816
Total Current Assets	1,423	1,082	1,125	1,009	1,192
Fixed assets less depreciation	217	223	220	221	214
Total assets	$1,640	$1,035	$1,345	$1,230	$1,406
Liabilities and Owners' Equity					
Payables and accruals	$ 562	$ 280	$ 249	$ 169	$ 199
Refunds due customers	63	63	63	63	67
Accrued income taxes	24	38	40	40	40
Notes payable to banks and others	344	251	68	31	181
Total Current Liabilities	993	632	420	303	487
Long-term notes payable	18	27	271	265	252
Total Liabilities	1,011	659	691	568	739
Owners' equity	629	646	654	662	667
Total liabilities and owner's equity	$1,640	$1,305	$1,345	$1,230	$1,406

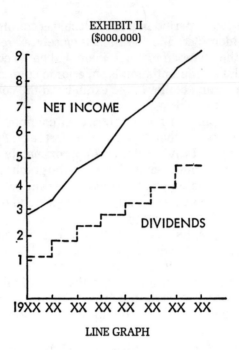

LINE GRAPH

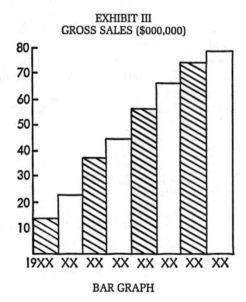

BAR GRAPH

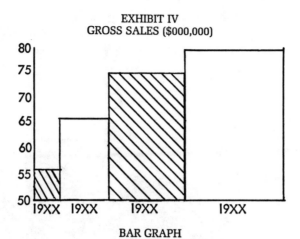

EXHIBIT IV
GROSS SALES ($000,000)

BAR GRAPH

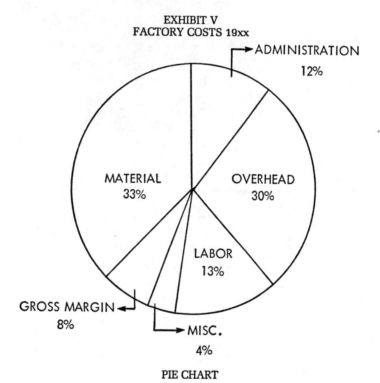

EXHIBIT V
FACTORY COSTS 19xx

PIE CHART

EXHIBIT VI
MAP OF WEST VIRGINIA SHOWING SALES TERRITORIES

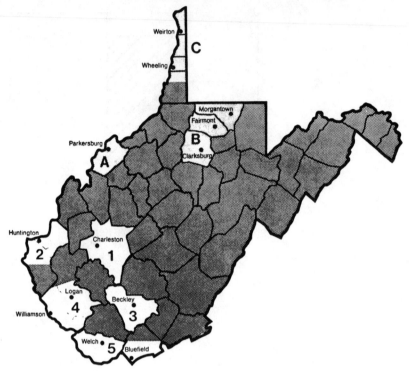

Existing Sales Territories

1 Kanawha County, Charleston City
2 Cabell & northern Wayne Counties, Huntington City
3 Raleigh County, Beckley City
4 Logan & Mingo Counties, Logan & Williamson Cities
5 McDowell & southern Mercer Counties, Welch & Bluefield Cities

Potential Sales Territories

A Wood County, Parkersburg City
B Monongalia, Marion, & Harrison Counties, Morgantown, Fairmont, & Clarksburg Cities
C Wheeling - Weirton area

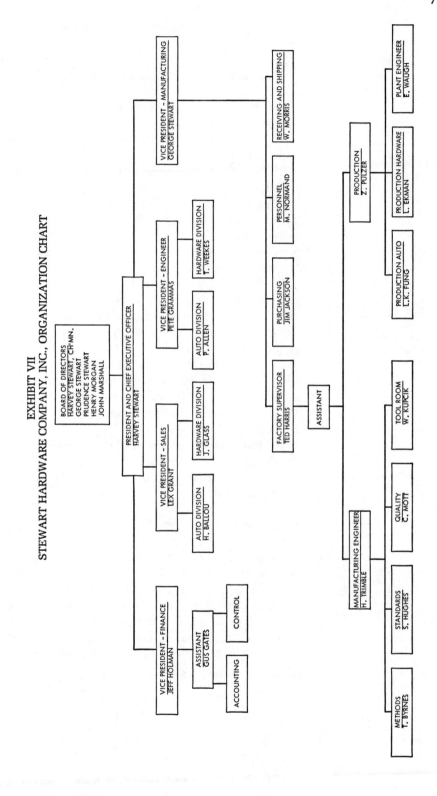

EXHIBIT VII
STEWART HARDWARE COMPANY, INC., ORGANIZATION CHART

one. If my mathematics is correct, the area of the last bar is 23 times the area of the first, yet sales have not even doubled. Dirty pool. Pevley Clip would fire you forthwith and good riddance.

Bars should be of the same width, scales should start at zero, and don't you dare to forget it!

4. Pie charts. See Exhibit V. These are effective when showing percentages that should add up to 100. Government and corporate reports are full of them. They tell us how every dollar received is spent, what portion of our food bill goes for groceries, meat, dairy products, and beer and hard liquor. Two problems arise when pie charts are constructed. If several segments are small, how do you label them? Writing sideways on the chart is hard to read, and a number of arrows pointing to mother-in-law slivers isn't good either. The other problem is mechanical. Twelve percent of a circle is 43.2 degrees. If you can mark off 43.2 degrees of arc, more power to you. If you can't, get someone who can or use a different kind of chart.

5. Map graphs. Refer to Exhibit VI for an example. Maps are a great help when readers are asked to visualize a geographic area. They must, however, be well drawn and accurate. Don't clutter the map with too much writing. Use shading, numbers, and letters with the keys printed below the map.

6. Organization charts. Instead of spending a page describing who reports to whom or where the director of stockholder relations fits into the corporate hierarchy, why not draw an organization chart? (See Exhibit VII.) Many times it helps to show the names of the individuals who occupy the boxes.

7. Floor plans—Flowcharts. A well-drawn floor plan of a proposed factory will impress the board more than a thousand descriptive words. Often the flow of material through a shop can be dramatically presented by showing the path it takes from department to department as it is being converted from raw material to finished product. (I must apologize. I had intended to use as an exhibit a plan of Pin-Up's new Shelbyville plant which shows how fourteen-inch logs are fabricated into clothespins in a continuous operation lasting only fifty-seven minutes; however, Pevley Clip confiscated the exhibit on the grounds it might divulge to the competition the secret methods of manufacturing that had made Pin-Up the leader in the clothespin industry.)

8. Glyphs. I'll bet you never heard of them. I hadn't until I read about the little things in a book. A glyph is a symbolic figure or character, a scratching. Thus, when I ask if you know what a glyph is, I should scribble a doodle after the question, and I have made a

glyph. "Profits were down last year. They will be up this year."

The author of the book exhorted his readers to use glyphs in visual aids prepared for speeches, to include them in exhibits and even to scatter them through the text of a report to lighten the atmosphere with a bit of humor. In my judgment he is a glyphomaniac, and though I am indebted to him for teaching me a new word, the three glyphs I have drawn will be my total production lifetimewise.

It is undesirable to have to turn a page sideways to read an exhibit, but sometimes this is unavoidable, as in Exhibit VII. Long sheets of paper are a pain in the neck for a reader to handle and so are exhibits that unfold to a width of a couple of feet and, like roadmaps, are impossible to refold in original creases. Both exhibits and reports should be written on the same size paper.

Properly used, exhibits can be substantial word savers, which may be important when there is a rigid limit to the length of a report.

Exhibits should be numbered in the order they are mentioned in the text. Reference to them may be made in two ways: "Exhibit I shows an estimated . . ." or "Profits of $100,000 are projected (Exhibit II)." Use Roman numerals when identifying exhibits. Exhibits should not be scattered through the text but should be grouped together at the end of the report.

FIRST THINGS FIRST

Don't get bogged down in details and nonessentials at the expense of ignoring major areas. A judicious use of an outline will aid a writer in avoiding this trap. Pin-Up's market has been seriously eroded by the increasing popularity of home dryers, and the company is considering the introduction of a silver-plated metallic pin in an attempt to dominate the top segment of the market. Pevley Clip instructs one of his assistants to write a report on the feasibility of the project. Amos Singlefoot shuns the assistance of an outline in organizing his report and assigns weights and values to the issues involved in these proportions:

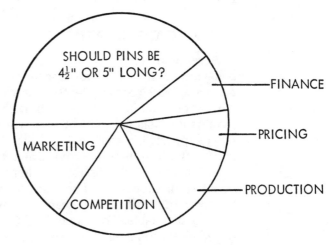

If we are charitable, we can say that Amos has sliced his pie all wrong. He has his priorities rear end up. The length of the pins is a detail, and it is debatable if Pin-Up will experience any substantial competition should it proceed with the project. On the other hand, it would appear that a market study of the proposal is essential. Will people buy silver-plated clothespins at the recommended price of $12.85 each? Indeed, is that the right price? How many does Pin-Up expect to sell? Can that number be turned out without upsetting production schedules of standard items? Is the company able to finance the new line? What is a realistic projection of the results in the first year? These are some of the basic questions that must be answered before design, sales, and production argue about the critical half-inch of length.

Some major areas may be covered adequately in a few sentences, whereas less important issues might require more explanation. Exhibits can be most helpful in cutting down demands for space in a report. Balance is the essential ingredient when a report is blocked out in the planning stage.

CONSISTENCY

Conclusions should flow from analysis, not move counter to it. A report should be internally consistent so that a statement made on page one is not reversed later on.

"Amos Singlefoot debauched my teenaged sister, purloined the family silver from his widowed and destitute mother, and burned the county poorhouse causing the deaths of forty senile octogenarians."

Three pages later the following sentence appears: "Amos Singlefoot is a man of integrity, possesses a sterling character, and is guided by the highest principles of ethical and moral conduct."

Note: The reason Amos is no longer a member of Pevley's personal staff or even an employee has nothing to do with certain irregularities of his character but because Clip held him responsible for the silver-plated pin debacle. Pevley's motto has always been "First things first."

IGNORING THE NEGATIVE

Accentuating the positive is an admirable characteristic of personal behavior, but it is not always the best policy in business circles. All too often a writer sweeps under the rug whatever unpleasant facts he happens upon if he finds they are not compatible with his neat and comfortable analysis and conclusions. He is prone to acknowledge only what supports his argument and ignore whatever does not. This tendency often results from arriving at a faulty conclusion.

In the best of all possible worlds a recommendation conceivably might fit all known facts and considerations. In our imperfect society, however, this will seldom occur, and trade-offs of various magnitude will be inevitable. For example, Pin-Up's decision to make silver-plated clothespins may be fully compatible with the company's capabilities with the exception that $800 will have to be expended to run new power lines to the plating tanks. This expense is acceptable when related to the expected profits of the project, but if it becomes evident that a new building must be constructed at a cost of $2 million to house the operation, that would put an entirely different complexion on the matter.

Even if the expenditure were determined to be economically sound, the question of the availability of the $2 million would have to be explored. Has Pin-Up the necessary cash, or can it borrow it? If the money can be obtained, is this the best possible use for it? All these questions would have to be answered before the final decision is made.

It does not pay to see only what you want to see and to consider only what reinforces your argument. Should there be too many loose ends left dangling and a number of embarrassing unanswered questions that must be ignored, the alarm buzzer should sound, and the writer should reexamine the validity of his analysis and conclusions.

Another ploy often used to get around a sticky point goes like this: "Since I have no information on factory capacity, I will assume Pin-Up has the facilities necessary to silver-plate three thousand clothespins an hour." The sentence makes innocuous reading, but the writer who attempts to whisk it by the nose of Pevley might find himself in the plating tanks along with his clothespins.

BREADTH OF ANALYSIS

There is a law of nature to the effect that every action is accompanied by an equal and opposite reaction. Also, there is a saying, the details of which are unclear to me, concerning irresistible forces and immovable objects. All this leads to the fact that when something happens, something else has got to give. Thus, when a business decision is made, the course of action undertaken may have a substantial effect on seemingly nonrelated matters.

For example, Pin-Up's plating tanks will be filled to capacity for ninety days with the new plated pins, and it will be impossible to platinum plate the twelve dozen gross of kitchen matches ordered by the Emir of Qhat, who will use them as a bribe to lure a French chef from the employ of the Maharajah of Rawalpindi. Failure to fill the Emir's order in timely fashion will possibly cause his cousin, the Caliph of Quot, to break off negotiations on the purchase of solid gold walking sticks for the twenty-two fathers of his forty-six wives.

It is essential to appraise the effect any decision might have on other activities of a company. Whether or not Pin-Up should produce silver-plated pins is an issue that must be evaluated in relation to the whole situation of the company. Much more is involved than the pins themselves.

Avoid superficiality. Analyze in depth and deal in specifics. There may be a single major component in a problem, but it is most unlikely that only a single issue needs to be handled. Don't limit coverage too narrowly. Breadth and depth of analysis are essential. The writer should develop his perception so he can see the whole situation, not just one narrow segment. The one-shot approach is usually the wrong one.

No decision can be made in a vacuum. The solution of one problem often creates other problems that must also be solved. Leander Wigglesworth, foreman of the plating department, demands an air-conditioned office so he can escape the malodorous fumes emanating from one of his plating tanks. It is given to him, and the day he moves in, seventeen other foremen petition for equal treatment.

Decisions should take into consideration the implications inherent in the recommended action. A broad view is necessary, and qualities of sensitivity and perception must be developed in order to anticipate the new problems that will arise so that solutions to them will be found along with the solution to the original problem. No problem or issue is an island unto itself.

PROOF BY MATHEMATICS

Very often a writer, carried away by his rhetoric and lost in a maze of mathematical computations of his own creation, reaches conclusions that are totally unrealistic. The mathematics may be perfect, but they might project a result that is ridiculous. Such an unfortunate situation arises when assumptions and analytical processes are basically unsound. Always examine decisions in the cold, hard light of common sense.

Let us assume that Pin-Up intends to test-market its silver-plated clothespins in Tupelo, Mississippi, and the adjacent area, which would include the teeming metropolises of Shannon, Fulton, Okolona, and Pontotoc. Let us also suppose that the gross margin per silver-plated pin is 85 cents and the costs of the special introductory program including advertising, promotion, special sales efforts, and substantial discounts to retailers add up to $963,333. Mathematics tells us that Pin-Up must sell 1,133,333 silver-plated pins to break even. No one can dispute the accuracy of the computations, but mastery of the fundamentals of addition, subtraction, multiplication, and division cannot alter the fact that the 19,000 men, women, and children of Tupelo, plus about another 20,000 in the outer environs of the city would have to purchase twenty-nine clothespins at $12.85 each for Pin-Up to meet its break-even point. It is highly probable that a number of children under the age of six, even if they had the necessary $372.65, would forego the purchase of silver-plated pins in favor of a Superman costume and two thousand dozen pieces of bubble gum.

Every conclusion should be tested against the hard facts of life. Any projections or course of action must be reasonable and realistic.

REASONABLE

What is reasonable? What is realistic? Is it a matter of personal intuitive judgment, a product of experience? "It is reasonable to expect a 5 percent increase in sales." "A cost increase of 4 percent is to be expected." "Historically, earnings have increased at 6 percent per annum, and it is reasonable to expect this trend to continue." All this is very persuasive. Who can argue about a modest 4 percent, 5 percent, or 6 percent? Any normal person would accept that on faith. Not so!

Remember this: Nothing happens unless something is done to cause it to happen. Pin-Up's silver-plated clothespins won't sell themselves even at 25 cents each. Some action must take place before a single pin is sold. Nothing is reasonable or realistic by fiat. It must be demonstrated to be reasonable or realistic before we can accept the conclusion. Reasonableness must be determined by analysis, not mandate.

DECISION MAKING

There is no place in reports for vague generalizations. Statements should be definite, specific, and must be clearly and precisely presented. "In order to meet corporate goals, Pin-Up must develop a strong marketing program." Such a statement is valueless unless the writer lays out in detail his "strong" plan. Specificity is essential. Who is to do what, when will he do it, and exactly how will it be done? A writer must be convincing and willing to take full responsibility for his decision. Decision is the name of the game, and an unwillingness to commit oneself wholeheartedly to a course of action is tantamount to abdication of the responsibilities and privileges of management.

Some persons are constitutionally unable to reach a decision and then act on it. To them there are not two sides to every question, but perhaps a dozen, and there is so much to be said in support of each approach that it is impossible to choose one above all the others. Such persons will undoubtedly find more happiness and success in philosophic milieus than as sales executives for Pin-Up Corporation.

In business the best decision or course of action is not always determinable. No man can bat a thousand in any league. As a matter of fact, not since 1941 has a major leaguer batted .400, and even then Ted Williams made out three times for every two hits he made. The main thing is he got the bat off his shoulder and took his cuts when he faced a pitcher. If an executive cannot be expected always to make the best decision, at least he can be expected not to make the worst, and as his perception and experience broaden, the quality of his decisions should improve. Don't be afraid to put your neck on the line. That is what necks are for, and how else can you expect to sell silver-plated clothespins?

Don't be afraid to make a mistake. Mistakes are normal and expected events, even in Pin-Up and other superlatively run companies. Strive for a good batting average, and let the chips fall where they may. However, the successful executive is perceptive enough to see a mistake soon after it has been made, man enough to acknowledge it, and capable enough to correct it before it destroys his company and himself.

Making decisions in reports is difficult because the writer goes on record, and he is aware his mistakes will return to haunt him. Consequently, his analysis must be complete, sound, and in depth so that the odds of being right are as much in his favor as he can make them.

BEING CONVINCING AND AT THE SAME TIME HONEST

An action report must be forceful, persuasive, and conclusive. Your analysis and recommendations may be absolutely perfect, but if your readers are not convinced, your recommendations will probably be ignored. Thus, it is not only what you say that is important but also how you say it. Style, organization of material, clarity, succinctness of expression, word choice—all these elements are factors in establishing credibility. Beautiful expression, however, cannot compensate for shallowness of argument. For best results, a combination of good form and sound analysis is recommended.

Reports generally are persuasive. The writer analyzes a situation and decides on the course of action he considers to be the best solution to the problem. Believing in the validity of his solution, he does his utmost to convince his readers to do what he recommends. If he is to earn a reputation for credibility and reliability, he must be scrupulously honest in every word he writes. Total honesty is an absolute requisite.

We have talked about unsupported assumptions regarded as facts, ignoring facts that do not fit into a solution, reaching unrealistic conclusions, and several other elements that weaken reports. Actually, many of these have to do with the personal integrity of the writer. Even though he may not be aware he is being less than candid, the effect of his faulty analysis may convince his reader to do something that is not in his best interest.

A writer must never fail to be aware of his responsibility to be honest and straightforward.

PRAGMATISM

Pin-Up's pugnacious panjandrum, Pevley Clip, prides himself on his no-nonsense attitude. Excerpts from his recent speech to the McMinnville Lions Club were printed in the local *Clarion*. "'Show me' is my slogan," Mr. Clip stated. "When someone tries to con me into something, I ask three questions: 'Says who? So what? Is that really so?' In my shop nobody, not nobody, pulls the wool over my eyes. I point the horny finger at them and they better have the right answers." The reporter added that as Mr. Clip roared these words, he extended his right arm stiffly and pointed his forefinger, curved like the cruelly hooked beak of a turkey buzzard, at his cringing audience.

Adoption of Pevley's attitude, if not his manner, can prove rewarding to all managers. Report writers, especially if their boss is a man like Clip, will be wise to make sure every statement they make is accurate, fully substantiated, clear, and realistic. At the same time their argument should be consistent and directed at the issues under discussion.

RISK

Decisions usually involve both rewards and risks. Swinging the bat is necessary if your desire is to hit a home run. At the same time, the batter cannot ignore the possibility he might strike out. Business executives are often extremely adept in evaluating the benefits that should accrue from a recommended course of action, but the most successful of them never ignores the risk side of the question. He asks and answers these questions: What could go wrong? What would be the cost if it did? How could the damage be controlled? What remedial action could be taken? Above all, he must have a realistic understanding of the probabilities of success or failure.

Amos Singlefoot might forecast $100,000 profit from silver-plated pins in the first year, but hard-nosed, pragmatic Pevley might decide there is only a 10 percent chance of this happening, whereas there is a 90 percent chance Pin-Up would lose up to $1 million on the project. The decision is reduced to an analysis of reward, exposure, probability. No report writer should fail to evaluate the risks involved when he recommends a course of action.

LAST WORDS IN THIS CHAPTER

At this time I have an almost irresistible urge to gather all the pearls of wisdom scattered so profusely through the preceding pages into a summary of startling clarity and brilliance. Remembering that reiteration is redundancy, I conquer the impulse and close with the last paragraph of the final report written to Clip by Amos Singlefoot. A small company was up for sale, and Clip asked Amos for specific recommendations covering: Should Pin-Up make an offer to buy, and, if so, how high should Pin-Up be prepared to go?

The following quotation is the conclusion of the report.

The important things to keep in mind when making your decision are: Clothes Horse is making a good profit and should continue to do so in the future: the price seems to be about right for the business: The dollar investment is well within your means, and there is every reason to believe that you can make a healthy return on this investment. This is as far as I can go, Mr. Clip: The rest is up to you.

When he finished reading, Pevley was so enraged he jotted down nine excerpts and noted his comments on each. He added a short note and sent the handwritten sheet and the report to Charley Lightfoot.

your decision.   —   I asked for his decision

good profit   —   How big is good?

should continue   —   Perhaps it should.
                             Will it?

Price seems to be   —   What price? Why does
about right   it seem right? What
                             does about mean?

Well within your   —   What are our means?
means

Every reason to   —   Not one reason not
believe   to believe?

Healthy return   —   What is healthy? $ ₵ ₵
                             is what I want.

As far as I can go   —   He hasn't gone anywhere,
                             yet.

Rest is up to you   —   Rest of it? He means all
                             of it.

                    Immediate Action!

Charley—
     Fire him. Pull whatever strings you have to but
get him a top job with the competition. Having him
working against us instead of for us guarantees a 10%
increase in our share of Market.   Cliff

---- QUIZ ----

Space is provided for your answers.

1. Exhibits. Why use them? What principles govern their use?

2. Name seven types of exhibits. Do you understand the use of all of them? If not, reread the exhibit section of the chapter.

Write a sentence or two on the following subjects.

3. Consistency.

4. Ignoring the negative.

5. Breadth of analysis.

6. Proof by mathematics.

7. Reasonable.

8. Decision making.

9. Honesty.

10. Risk.

ANSWERS

1. Exhibits explain, clarify, support, and supplement the text of a report.
   Facts disclosed in exhibits should be stated in the text which must stand independent of exhibits, so it is not necessary to check exhibits to understand the text. Exhibits, too, must be self-sufficient. It should not be necessary to consult the text in order to understand an exhibit.

2. a. Figures—balance sheets, profit and loss statements, tables, and so forth.
   b. Line graphs.
   c. Bar graphs.
   d. Pie charts.
   e. Map graphs.
   f. Organization charts.
   g. Floor plans, flow charts, engineering drawings.
3. Conclusions should flow from analysis, not run counter to it.
4. Unpleasant inconsistencies may not be swept under the rug. If too many exist, it is a signal that analysis and conclusions are faulty.
5. Analysis must be broad and deep. Actions cause counter actions. Each must be explored before a final decision is reached.
6. An answer may be correct mathematically speaking, but could arrive at an unrealistic or ridiculous conclusion. Check all results in the cold hard light of common sense.
7. Nothing is reasonable by fiat. Reasonableness is determined by analysis, not by mandate.
8. Decision making is the name of the game. Making some mistakes is inevitable but the key to success is the batting average. Keep yours high by deep and careful analysis before coming to a conclusion.
9. Honesty isn't the best policy, it is the *only* policy. Beware of unsupported assumptions regarded as facts, ignoring facts that do not fit conclusions, reaching unrealistic conclusions. They affect a writer's reputation for absolute integrity.
10. Never forget that every prospect of reward is accompanied by risk. Analysis of both reward and risk is essential. So is study of the probabilities associated with the broad spectrum of possible outcomes.

CONCLUSION

I commend you for your dedication and patience. A portion of what I have written may have provided heavy going for you—I suppose some frustration was inevitable—but I have endeavoured to make my style as readable and lighthearted as I could.

Basically, letters, memos, and reports are facts of life to a business person. They cannot be ignored. Yet, a knowledge of the principles involved in the writing of them should simplify the production process and make the finished product more effective.

If I have helped you to approach these desirable goals more closely, the expenditure of my time as well as yours has been amply repaid.

Good luck, and my best wishes to you.

W. G. Ryckman

EXAMINATIONS

EXAMINATION 1: CHAPTERS 1–3

1. Correct the following sentences if you find a word or words misused.
   a. A liter holds less ounces than a quart.

   b. Its fall and on the gridiron running backs elude tacklers.

   c. He was endowed with high ethical principals.

   d. Since both of us were gentlemen we reached an unwritten verbal agreement.

   e. His illegal escapades made him notorious.

   f. Watson was playing really good today.

2. Replace words that are incorrectly used.
   a. He literally fell flat on his face.

   b. I divided the money equally among John and Mary.

   c. At some point in time we must reduce expenditures.

   d. Rising postal charges have heavily impacted mail order companies.

   e. Eternal vigilance is necessary if we are to cut costs.

   f. The problem, i.e., what to do with excess stock, demands a solution to it.

3. Correct these sentences, if necessary.
   a. Every person in the world should count their blessings.

   b. At the present point in time unemployment is high.

   c. He and his brother are exactly identical twins.

   d. The housing development will cost nine million dollars over the next 3 years.

   e. 1492 was the date of Columbus' discovery of America.

   f. Irregardless of what you say, women are different than men in enjoyment of contact sports.

g. I question his ability to competently run the business.

h. It is my considered opinion that attention should be given the matter by the board.

4. What is wrong with the following passage? Correct what you can and raise questions on other points. Space is allowed for your answer.

It is my absolute conviction that something must be done about the situation by the engineering department. This is not normal, and they are fully responsible. To fully understand the problem, design engineers must get in to it. Also, it has been discovered that sales of hardware is slipping in Minnesota.

EXAMINATION 1 ANSWERS

1. a. Fewer.
   b. It's.
   c. Principles.
   d. Oral.
   e. Correct.
   f. Well.
2. a. Correct, provided he actually did fall flat on his face—not his chest—but can one fall *flat* on a lumpy object such as a face. Why not eliminate *literally*? Falling flat on one's face evokes a clear image to all of us without the confusing modifier.
   b. Between.
   c. *At some time, soon,* or even *We must reduce expenditures now.* Depends on what is meant.
   d. Affected.
   e. Alertness.
   f. Awful! Redundant, Latin abbreviation, sentence ending with a preposition. Also, is it the problem that demands a solution, or must we do something about excess stock? Why not: *We must decide what to do about excess stock.*
3. a. His.
   b. Now.
   c. Flush *exactly*—redundant.
   d. Three—consistency.
   e. Columbus discovered American in 1492.
   f. Regardless—different from.
   g. I question his ability to run the business competently.
   h. I believe the board should consider the matter.

4. What a dog. Nearly everything is wrong.
    a. *It is my absolute conviction.* Bad, too dogmatic. Replace with *I believe.*
    b. *Something must be done.* Weak—passive voice. Rephrase: *The engineering department must do something about the situation.*
    c. I don't like the vague *something.* The writer doesn't tell us what is wrong and what should be done about it. He should have.
    d. *This* is vague. To what is the writer referring? *This* what?
    e. If *they* refers to the engineering department the pronoun should be *it.* Department is singular, and the pronoun should agree.
    f. *To fully understand.* Split infinitive. You could replace with *to understand fully,* but there is still double use of the word *fully.* Rewrite: *For complete understanding of the problem.*
    g. Who is supposed to *understand fully?* Management (the writer of the memo), the engineering department, or the design engineers? Let the writer say what he means, provided he has any idea what he is trying to say.
    h. *Must get in to it.* Awful. In the first place *in to* should be *into,* but even then the sentence is awkward and ends with a preposition. Rewrite. *For (management) to understand the problem, the design engineers should. . . .* Tell them precisely what they should do—check the specifications, recalculate stresses, whatever is required. Be specific.
    i. Last sentence violates one-point principle for paragraphs. Start a new paragraph.
    j. *It has been discovered.* Weak passive construction. Who discovered it? Tell us.
    k. Sales is plural. *Sales are slipping.* The verb refers to sales, not hardware.

How many of these points did you catch? Did you discover any that I missed?

EXAMINATION 2: CHAPTERS 4–5

Space is provided for your answers.

1. Audience, role, assignment. Discourse on these subjects as they affect report writing.

2. What are your thoughts on stating your recommendations at the beginning of an action report?

3. Exhibits. List do's and don't's in preparing them. Explain why good is good and bad is bad.

4. "No problem or issue is an island unto itself." A paragraph or two on this, please.

5. Please write your thoughts on specificity as related to report writing.

EXAMINATION 2 ANSWERS

1. The writer's attitude should be established by his analysis of the audience he will be addressing. The position of the individuals he is writing to will influence his style; so will their familiarity with the subject matter.

    Awareness of his role will also influence a writer. Is he a teacher, explainer, persuader? His attitude will be in keeping with his purpose. If he is an acknowledged expert in the field, he will be careful not to overpower his readers with unfamiliar technical terms if they are not equal experts.

    He will never be unaware of his assignment and he will adhere precisely to it, avoiding extraneous matters and confining himself to the issues under discussion.

2. It is extremely wise to put final recommendations in the opening paragraph of an action report. If the reader knows the answer as he begins to read, he will be able to test evidence, every statement made in the report, against the known conclusion. Knowing where you, the writer, are going will help the reader to follow your argument, and he will be ready for each step you make in developing your argument.

    If your recommendations are saved for the last paragraph, it will be difficult for the reader to follow the trend of your analysis as he reads.

3. Exhibits should be:
    a. Clear, simple—otherwise, who could understand what they attempt to demonstrate?
    b. Self-sufficient, self-explanatory—so that no instructions for understanding them will appear in text.
    c. Numbered consecutively in order of appearance in text—Don't make it difficult for reader by starting with Exhibit III and then skipping to Exhibit I.
    d. Honest—Don't attempt to prove unprovable points by manipulating scales on horizontal and vertical axes.
    e. Conforming in position on page—Try not to force reader to turn pages sideways except when there is no alternative.
    f. Prepared using differentiated lines, for example, one solid, another dotted—Do not confuse a reader if lines cross.
    g. Neatly and accurately drawn—for the general impression on the reader and to make sure he is not left with an erroneous opinion.

    Exhibits should not be:
    a. Excessively cluttered—Exhibits with too much information confuse rather than clarify.
    b. Prepared on anything except standard size pages—Long sheets are an abomination. Excessively wide sheets defy refolding. Violate these principles only when compelled to by dire necessity.
    c. So involved that a page of text must be devoted to explain methodology of preparation or provide instruction as to how to

interpret—Exhibits should "stand on their own two feet" so a reader can grasp their message even if he studies them before he reads the text.

4. No decision can be made in a vacuum. Every action causes an equal but opposite reaction, and the solution of one problem will often create other problems that must be assessed before one embarks on a course of action.

    Every action is accompanied by risks, and a solution must also contain remedies for the risks created by the solution. These remedies, too, may cause further problems, and they must also be solved. Analysis should be thorough, even to the third or fourth generation of problems.

    The bane of the life of an executive is surprises. Avoid them by doing your homework before you commit your company to a course of action. Weigh the total risks against the expected rewards.

5. Avoid vague generalizations in reports. Statements should be definite, specific, and ought to be precisely stated. If action is to be taken, the exact steps should be set forth. The individual responsible for action should be named, and a time limit should be established for performance of the project. No stones should be left unturned; everything should be nailed down in unequivical terms. Don't allow the occasion to arise when someone can say, "I'm sorry, but I thought so-and-so was going to do that." Remember the newspaperman's dictum: who, what, when, where, how.

INDEX